Germany
UNRAVELING AN ENIGMA

GREG NEES

INTERCULTURAL PRESS
A Nicholas Brealey Publishing Company

BOSTON • LONDON

First published by Intercultural Press, a Nicholas Brealey
Publishing Company, in 1999. For information contact:

Intercultural Press, Inc.
a division of
Nicholas Brealey Publishing
20 Park Plaza, Suite 1115A
Boston, MA 02116, USA
Tel: (+) 617-523-3801
Fax: (+) 617-523-3708
www.interculturalpress.com

Nicholas Brealey Publishing
3–5 Spafield St., Clerkenwell
London, EC1R 4QB, UK
Phn: + 44-(0) 207-239-0360
Fax: + 44-(0) 207-239-0370
www.nicholasbrealey.com

ISB-13: 978-1-877864-75-9
ISBN-10: 1-877864-75-7

Printed in the United States of America

12 11 10 09 08   8 9 10 11 12

Library of Congress Cataloging-in-Publication Data

Nees, Greg.
    Germany: unraveling an enigma/Greg Nees.
       p. cm.
    Includes bibliographical references and index.
    ISBN 1-877864-75-7
       1. National characteristics, German.   2. Germany—
    Ethnic relations.   3. Public opinion—Germany.
    4. Germany—Social conditions—1990- .   5. Ger-
    many—Social life and customs—20th century.   I. Title.
    DD76 N38 2000
    305.8'00943—dc21   99-046629

W

Germany

The InterAct Series
Other books in the series:
AU CONTRAIRE! FIGURING OUT THE FRENCH
BORDER CROSSINGS: AMERICAN INTERACTIONS WITH ISRAELIS
BUENOS VECINOS
A COMMON CORE: THAIS AND AMERICANS
ENCOUNTERING THE CHINESE
EXPLORING THE GREEK MOSAIC
A FAIR GO FOR ALL: AUSTRALIAN/AMERICAN INTERACTIONS
FROM *DA* TO YES: UNDERSTANDING THE EAST EUROPEANS
FROM *NYET* TO *DA*: UNDERSTANDING THE RUSSIANS
GOOD NEIGHBORS: COMMUNICATING WITH THE MEXICANS
INTO AFRICA
LEARNING TO THINK KOREAN
MODERN-DAY VIKINGS
SPAIN IS DIFFERENT
UNDERSTANDING ARABS: A GUIDE FOR WESTERNERS
UNDERSTANDING SPANISH-SPEAKING SOUTH AMERICANS
WITH RESPECT TO THE JAPANESE

Greg Nees is available as a trainer/consultant on the subjects covered in this book. He can be reached at:
e-mail: greg@german-connection.com
Phone: 720-494-8813
Fax: 720-494-8814

To my family, for teaching me about the essentials of life and motivating me to go further. And for my friends, lovers, and teachers who have supported me in that quest.

Table of Contents

x

To the Reader

As hard as I have tried to be objective, this book cannot be without its biases, however subtle they may be. Many might find this unfortunate, but it is now accepted among most competent scholars and social scientists that our cultural mindset affects all our perceptions and opinions about human society. What this means, in effect, is that everyone's point of view is only just that, a point of view. No one observer can claim the privilege of viewing and understanding other humans or groups from an absolutely valid position that does not inherently contain subjective biases. While this realization may be disturbing for some, the inherent subjectivity of our perceptions does not give us as authors carte blanche to write or say whatever we choose. On the contrary, it makes thorough research, openness about methods, and a willingness to be as explicit as we can about both our point of view and our motives all the more necessary.

One brief paragraph, then, about my methods. Before beginning my data collection in Germany, I reviewed much of the literature available on German history, culture, business, and customs. I also looked at scholarly articles comparing the United States and Germany along various dimensions. As part of my dissertation research, I spent ten months in Germany during 1994 and 1995. During this time I conducted an extensive series of interviews with friends, acquaintances, and strangers, both in personal and professional settings. Further data was generated by my active participation and observation in many spheres of German life. After collecting the data and using it to write my dissertation, I continued using my various cross-cultural seminars to collect additional information and also continued to read extensively on the subject.

All of this information I "distilled" through my own set of subjective filters through which I perceive the world. Such filters greatly influence my worldview, as I believe they do all human beings. Rather than pretend we don't operate with personal filters, as good scholars I believe we should strive for higher self-awareness of what our biases actually are. To this end, I would like to offer the reader some idea of how my own filters developed during both my childhood and my resocialization in Germany.

My point of view might best be described as "trans-Atlantic." By that I mean that I perceive myself as a member of both the American and German cultures. I was born in eastern Pennsylvania in 1949 of working-class German and Anglo-Saxon ancestors. I grew up thinking of myself as a "normal, freedom-loving American male," but this area of Pennsylvania contains some strong cultural currents left over from the early German immigrants who arrived there. These influenced me more than I was aware of.

For me this German background was like a ghost in my life. I rarely noticed it at first. I was more interested in girls, sports, and cars; there was little space in my life for any serious reflection. But this influence was always there, although often invisible. While I sometimes puzzled about who the Germans were, I didn't really give it much thought. But the older I got, the more the question troubled me. Did they resemble the characters on television programs like *Hogan's Heroes* or were they more like the Nazi storm troopers I saw in films that were partially documentary and partially propaganda? Or were they people like my grandparents whom I loved so dearly?

Perhaps my grandfather personified this mystery the most for me. Although he was born in the United States, his family was pure German and he grew up bilingual. That was not uncommon in those days in Lancaster, Pennsylvania, which is where he lived. He was a gentle, hardworking man who would sacrifice anything for his family. He loved nothing more than to visit with friends and family and to talk and tell jokes, especially with his grandchildren.

But he experienced World War I as an American soldier fighting against the Germans, and this scarred him deeply. Although he had served honorably, he always avoided talking about that war—perhaps for the same reason he would never speak German to any of his children or grandchildren. This always seemed odd to me, because I later learned he spoke German as fluently as he spoke English. Sometimes I would catch him conversing with his brothers in German, but he quickly switched to English when he noticed me. Only later as an adult, after I experienced for myself what military life is like and began to grasp the grim horrors of war, could I understand more of what he must have felt.

This mysterious question about who and what the Germans were bothered me enough that in 1976 I decided to answer it by planning a trip around the world. In my youthful naiveté, I planned a tour of Europe, including a stop in Germany for a few months. I thought that would be enough time to get to the bottom of the culture question, and then I could continue on through Africa and Asia to cross the Pacific and return to California.

Life had its own plans for me, however, and I ended up spending thirteen years in Germany, years that were exciting, challenging, and enriching. During this time I learned the language, becoming fluent enough to study at a German university, and began what would be a long exploration of the complexities of cultures. After graduation, I worked as both a translator and a language instructor. I immersed myself in the culture to such an extent that people who didn't know me rarely realized I was an American. In effect, I "went native." I rarely spoke English, and the majority of my friends and acquaintances were Germans. I had learned to live and think like many of my German friends, and, surprisingly, I enjoyed it. After the first difficult years of transition, I felt very comfortable, and the longer I stayed, the more difficult it was to leave.

When I finally did return to the United States in 1990, both the world and I had changed immensely. Reverse culture shock soon made it clear that I was no longer the same "normal American" I was when I left. I was surprised how hard it was to integrate myself back into my country of origin. Paradoxically, I realized that I was now an insider and outsider to both American and German cultures. At first I felt like the character in A Man without a Country, but as I began to reintegrate and adjust, I began to develop what I have learned to call my "trans-Atlantic" point of view.

This ability to be an insider and outsider in both countries has helped me grow personally as well as allowed me to use my knowledge and experiences professionally, both as a cross-cultural trainer and as a facilitator for multicultural groups and organizations. Being insider and outsider to two cultures does not mean I am neutral or objective, but it does mean I am better able to understand the views and biases of both sides and serve as a sort of human bridge.

And that is what I have tried to do in this book: to offer Americans an insider's exploration of the German mindset and culture. I have tried to do this in a way that both Germans and Americans will find valid and acceptable. This has been a challenge. Looking at the world from another culture's perspective causes us discomfort, as it invariably brings many of our biases to light and calls into question assumptions that we have always taken for granted. But while this process is sometimes uncomfortable, if we are open to it, it also helps us grow as human beings and enlarges our world. I hope you, the reader, will find this book enlightening and valuable in your attempts to understand another part of what is truly becoming a global village. I also hope you will forgive whatever biases you may detect, knowing that I, like everyone, perceive the world through my own culturally influenced filters.

Acknowledgments

While many, many people have helped me in various ways to finish this book, I would like to acknowledge a few of those major contributors without whose help the project never would have been completed. Professors Heinz Göhring and Kristine Fitch have inspired and guided me in the field of intercultural communication in general and with my examination of German-American differences in particular. In addition Sylvia Schroll-Machl, Professor Alexander Thomas, and Professor Rolf Endres provided important insights and suggested useful avenues of further research. Sabine Amend helped immensely with research during the rewriting process, and Dr. Klaus Ufer, Adolf Diefenhardt, Dr. Reinhard Stolle, and Dr. Tilo Weber were crucial in offering detailed feedback and constructive criticism to various versions of the original manuscript.

Numerous friends, acquaintances, and seminar participants supported the long process of research and data collection by allowing me detailed interviews on their insiders' view of the German way of life, as well as by offering moral support along the way. Among others, they include Peter Boback, Ute Iding-Doll and Dr. Martin Doll, Petra Siegmann, Sabine Bussmann-Barrios, Willi Breitner, Rudiger Schuckert, Frank Steinmeier, Almut Simmchen-Ovie, Dr. Volker Radtke, Dr.

Henning Wienand, Hedi Pruy-Lange, Dr. Stefanie Lindstaedt, Dr. Wolfgang Lindstaedt, and Elisabeth Schnellinger. Special thanks to Carlos Barrios and Alex Uslar for crucial emotional and logisitical support.

I am also very indebted to Dr. George Renwick, who originally suggested I take my ideas for this project to Intercultural Press, without whom this book would not exist. In particular, my editor, Judy Carl-Hendrick, deserves special thanks for teaching me much about good writing and helping transform an information-rich manuscript into the book you now have before you. Needless to say, any errors are my own.

Introduction

The Germans are an enigma not only to the rest of the world but also to themselves. Why does a society that prizes security and order and that seems to have a rule for everything not set a speed limit on its superhighways, despite the increasingly high number of automobiles that use these roads? How does such a heavily regulated society manage to attain such economic success in the competitive global market? How could a culture that produced such inspired musicians and artists as Bach, Beethoven, Goethe, and Schiller and such profound philosophers and scientists as Kant, Hegel, Heisenberg, and Einstein fall prey to the barbarities of the Nazis? How can a people be so sentimental, loyal, and trustworthy on the one hand and be so arrogant and easy to dislike on the other? These are only some of the questions that people pose when they try to understand the Germans. But foreigners are not the only ones who have that difficulty.

Libraries and bookstores in Germany are filled with works attempting to answer these and other questions. Germans spend great amounts of time among themselves discussing their puzzling heritage and culture. In fact, as will become evident in chapter 4, discussing almost anything is one of the Germans' favorite pastimes. And trying to answer the question "What does it mean to be German?" is one of the more common topics in these discussions.

A legendary German hero offers some initial clues to this challenging puzzle. In the Teutoburger Forest near Detmold stands a huge metal statue of Hermann the Cheruscan, whom Roman historians called Arminius. According to history and legend, in A.D. 9 Hermann led the Cheruscans and other Germanic tribes in their crucial victory over the three Roman legions that were trying to conquer the territory which we have come to know as Germany. After this defeat, the Romans never again tried to invade the Germanic territories.

We know of this battle first because it was recorded by the Romans and second because it passed into legend among the Germanic tribes, who were an oral people. It resurfaced in the works of German authors and thinkers after the Middle Ages. But not until the nineteenth century did the romantic and nationalist forces choose to resurrect the legend as a symbol of the greatness of the Germanic peoples and their culture. During this period the huge, heroic statue of Hermann was constructed and his legend promulgated in German schools. And it was during this same period that Germany was united as a modern nation-state. Here we find a major piece in the German puzzle: why did it take this two-thousand-year-old culture until 1871 to finally coalesce into a modern nation?

The spread of the Hermann legend and the building of the great statue were outward symbols of a struggle for the construction of a national German identity and a modern German state. As such, they served as an antidote to the sense of insecurity and inferiority which has marked much of German history. This sense of insecurity was derived in part from Germany's geographic position, which often led to the Germanic kingdoms serving as battlefields where other European states fought their wars. It arose from watching other peoples—French, British, Spanish—form centralized states and create huge empires and great civilizations while the

Germanic states remained fragmented, with little political and economic clout. The Germans, divided into hundreds of small kingdoms, duchies, and principalities, felt themselves to be less than important in the grand scheme of Europe and the world. This lack of identity and sense of inferiority partly explains the preference of many of the German nobility for speaking and writing Latin during the Middle Ages and then French in later periods. It also prompted Emperor Charles V to say that the German language was only fit for speaking to horses.[1]

Today this feeling of inferiority lingers among the Germans. The atrocities of the Third Reich have only served to make it more difficult than ever for Germans to identify themselves as such. It is telling that many young Germans have little or no knowledge of their Germanic ancestors. When asked, they often don't even know who Hermann the Cheruscan was. And when queried about their ancient Germanic ancestors, they will usually say that they were a primitive and barbaric people who were neither literate nor capable of creating the infrastructure which made Rome such a great civilization. Given this negative prejudice toward their own ancestors, it is striking that among the New Age movement in Germany there are numerous Germans who are fascinated with Native American cultures. While traveling through Germany, you can occasionally catch sight of an Indian teepee in someone's backyard. You will also hear of groups of people gathering in sweat lodges or participating in other Native American religious rituals. It is ironic that Germans can be so fascinated by Native American cultures but have no interest in their own, when both cultures had so much in common—politically, culturally, and spiritually.

Many of us think we know quite a lot about the Germans. After all, we argue, they are not so different from us and they played a large part in our own history. More Germans immigrated to the United States than any other ethnic group, and approximately fifty million American citizens currently claim to be at least part German.[2] But our views of Germans are often skewed, especially by the media. Of course we know of the beer-drinking Germans in their traditional costumes at the Oktoberfest, and we know Germans make great cars, but the Nazi image is omnipresent for many Americans, even if only in the background. What would Indiana Jones have done without the Nazis to fight against? And how many of the villains in Hollywood films have had a German accent or worn uniforms similar to those of the Nazis?

Many of these images have become classic stereotypes, and as such they influence our perceptions, thoughts, and behaviors when dealing with Germans. The insidious thing about such stereotypes is that they often have a core of truth, which is then applied indiscriminately so that every German becomes like the stereotype. In addition to the loss of individuality that such pigeonholing brings with it, there is usually an implicit emotional judgment about the stereotype, which makes successful communication difficult.

The reader is advised to remember that Germany is a densely populated country of over eighty million people who exhibit considerable diversity, which includes regional differences and dialects, educational and class differences, and political and ideological differences. Like so many European countries, the spectrum of political thought and party allegiance in Germany is far wider than that found in the United States. A typical German will notice little political diversity in the United States and view the Democrats and Republicans as representing two flanks of the same party. Americans have little to compare with major political positions taken by the Social Democratic Party (SPD) or the Green Party, and this is significant in understanding the German worldview.

In this book I have attempted to find the broader, underlying patterns of German life and culture. In doing so I often talk about "the Germans" and "the Americans," realizing full well that such generalizations can slip easily into stereotypes.

Generalizations are useful, however, when trying to describe the overall form and structure of the forest without getting lost in the individual trees.

An illustration will make this clearer. While identifying Asian cultures as indirect has become a popular cliché, researchers have discovered there are differences in levels of directness among European cultures as well. Americans often pride themselves on how they "like to get to the point" and how they don't waste time "beating around the bush." From this perspective, the indirectness of Asians and their preoccupation with giving and saving face seems confusing and tedious, if not downright dishonest.

It thus comes as a surprise to many Americans to discover that the Germans are even more direct and less concerned about face issues than Americans are. As will be shown in the chapter on communication styles, this difference can cause significant problems when Americans and Germans try to communicate. Thus, while it makes sense to talk about the degree to which Germans and Americans are similar in their directness, in reality we find a great deal of difference in directness between these two cultures. There are some Americans who are blunter and more direct than most Germans, and there are some Germans who are very indirect. But this does not make the overall generalization any less valid if we assume that there is a normal distribution in both groups regarding this trait. Illustrated graphically, this distribution resembles three overlapping bell-shaped curves:

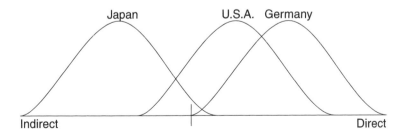

Japan   U.S.A. Germany

Indirect   Direct

Note that while both peak on the right-hand side of the continuum between indirectness and directness, the American peak is a little closer to the indirectness pole than the German. The peak, of course, is where you find the predominant pattern of behavior in that culture. Finally, note how much further the Japanese are toward the indirectness extreme than either Germans or Americans.

A last point: to avoid confusion and offense, let me explicitly state that when referring to "the Americans," I am speaking about the predominantly white, middle-class, mainstream culture within the United States. This is not to disavow the importance and richness of cultural variety within the U.S., but only to help draw a broad and easy-to-understand picture for the purposes of comparing and contrasting the two cultures.

---

[1] Gordon A. Craig, *The Germans* (New York: New American Library, 1983), 311.

[2] Don H. Tolzmann, "The German American Legacy," *German Life* 1, June/July, 1994, 46–49.

2

Who Are the Germans?

Germany is a complicated country, a fact the Germans themselves are first to acknowledge. To talk simplistically about German culture is to engage in verbal sleight of hand. The very idea of "German culture" is ambiguous because it can be understood on several levels. Do we mean the culture of the relatively young German nation, whose borders have changed several times in the last hundred years, or do we mean the culture of all the German-speaking peoples? The latter would have to include the Austrians, the great majority of the Swiss, and isolated groups of Germans as far east as the Volga and as far south as the Seven Mountains region of Romania, not to mention the German-speaking people in Alsace-Lorraine and Luxembourg.

For the sake of clarity, when used in this book *Germany* and *Germans* will refer exclusively to the Federal Republic of Germany and its citizens. But even by limiting this examination to the current culture of the Federal Republic of Germany, a surprising amount of complexity still remains. Although Germany is small by American standards—its total area is less than that of Montana—the diversity and complexity of this country are not to be underestimated. Understanding this complexity is a key to working, living, and communicating successfully with the Germans.

Modern Germany can be likened to a patchwork quilt that has been carefully sewn together from scores of different little kingdoms and principalities. To understand how this came to be and what its current consequences are, we must take a brief look at its history.

The Essentials of Modern German History

Americans are a forward-looking people who tend to orient more to the future than the past, and for that reason I have tried to keep the section on German history short. But it is useful to note that Germans take a different approach to history than do Americans. They tend to always look to historical precedents in order to understand the present, a perspective followed to some extent in this book. I often use German history as the context for the present. For that reason, it is wise for Americans to spend some time learning more about Germany's past.

Although many Americans show little interest in understanding or talking about history, this attitude is counterproductive when dealing with Germans. As will be described in greater detail in chapter 4, conversing and, in particular, engaging in detailed discussions are favorite national pastimes in Germany. Educated Germans have been raised to think and analyze historically; the American who learns the rudiments of this way of thinking and talking will earn respect and credibility from them.[1] Not to do so is to run the risk of being written off as simply another uneducated American who is ignorant of the more important things in life.

The English word *Germany* derives from the name *Germanus*, given to the people of this territory by Tacitus, an ancient Roman historian. Tacitus was quite taken by these early, seminomadic "Germanic" tribes, seeing in them a healthy, more natural way of life that he hoped would be an antidote for the decadence of the Roman Empire. The interesting fact is that none of these tribes called themselves "Germans."

After playing a major role in the downfall of the Roman Empire, these tribes were conquered by Charlemagne and converted to Christianity. Both the French and the Germans claim him as a national hero, but to the French he is Charlemagne and to the Germans, Karl der Große. Charlemagne was responsible for forcibly converting the last of the Germanic tribes to Christianity, and he also became emperor of the Holy Roman Empire in A.D. 800, uniting most of western and central Europe.

Within decades after his death, however, this empire began fragmenting politically, a process that continued for centuries. This was further encouraged by the religious wars following the Reformation. Fragmentation was to a large extent the result of Germanic laws of inheritance, which divided a man's property equally among his sons, in contrast to other European countries, where, under primogeniture, property passed in toto to the eldest son. Consequently, what would become Germany remained a weak network of small warring states rather than a strong centralized country like France, England, or Spain. In fact, in 1648, with the signing of the Peace of Westphalia, which ended the Thirty Years War, what would later become united Germany was then a jigsaw puzzle of approximately three hundred small autonomous kingdoms, duchies, principalities, and free cities. It was Prussia's destiny to change this.

Imperial Germany (1871–1918)

At the time of the Peace of Westphalia, Prussia was a small, unimportant kingdom located near present-day Berlin. But through a series of strategic wars, it expanded both its territory and power. Like Catholic Austria to the south, Protestant Prussia had designs on full control over the other German-speaking states. After a series of wars in which first Denmark, then Austria, and finally France were defeated, Prussia gained control over the German-speaking states, except for Switzerland and Austria. In 1871, under the leadership of the Prussian chancellor Otto von Bismarck, the German Empire was created, finally bringing about a unified Germany. Bismarck supported and guided the Industrial Revolution in Germany, helping this newly centralized state rapidly become a modern world power. Prussia's dominance left its mark on Germany in many ways, not the least of which is the fact that Berlin became the political center of modern Germany.

Like much of Europe, Prussia was organized according to a rigid hierarchy, which was basically a type of caste system. This class system was a direct outgrowth of European feudalism, an impediment against the democratic forces that were gaining strength throughout the continent and one of Bismarck's greatest political challenges. To deflate the growth of democracy and socialism, Bismarck created Germany's social insurance system, which is still in effect. This system serves as a major foundation for the social market economy that underpins German society. It is a major cultural component which reflects the Germans' traditional acceptance of the role of the guardian state and the consequent deemphasis on individual freedom. While many of Bismarck's policies had positive effects, which are still evident, his foreign policies, in particular his humiliating defeat of the French in 1871, set the stage for Germany's traumatic experiences in this century.

Many Americans are under the impression that Germany is solely responsible for starting World War I. This view ignores the complexities of European politics at the turn of the twentieth century. European countries were involved in a series of "entangling alliances"—some of them the result of Bismarck's policies—and thus were poised on the brink of war for several years before its actual outbreak in 1914. Experts agree that if the war had not started because of Germany's support of Austria (which declared war on Serbia), another trigger would have been pulled by the European powers to start the war they were all preparing for. In the end,

Germany's loss of this war gave France the opportunity to avenge itself for its defeat by the Prussians.

Weimar Republic (1918–1933)

After Germany's defeat and with American consent, the French and British governments declared Germany to be solely responsible for the outbreak of the war and imposed huge war reparations. This strategy was designed to cripple the economy and ensure that Germany would remain a second-rate power. After the enormous hardships and great personal sacrifice during the war years, the loss of World War I was a great blow for the Germans and had repercussions throughout the country. In November of 1918, as the war drew to a close, the German emperor, Wilhelm II, abdicated and fled the country. The official class system collapsed, and political views became polarized. Radical forces of both the left (communists and socialists) and the right (nationalists and monarchists) were armed and intent upon installing a government of their own choosing. These forces clashed violently in the larger cities, and civil war seemed about to engulf the nation.

During this period, a more moderate, democratic government was installed in the German city of Weimar. Elections were held, but while much of the outright street violence abated, political assassinations continued. The huge war reparations payments, designed to economically bleed the country, proved effective. Hyperinflation ravaged Germany, and, at its peak, prices doubled daily, creating further hardship and turmoil among the German populace.[2] Lifetime savings were wiped out overnight, and the economy collapsed, creating devastating unemployment. Finally, just when Germany seemed to be regaining some economic control, the stock market crashed in New York, setting off a worldwide economic depression.

This depression threw millions of Germans out of work and again set the stage for the emergence of small, radical political parties that could not agree on a common economic or political solution to Germany's problems. It was during this time that right-wing radicals reemerged and made their successful bid for power. By 1933 these radicals, in the form of the National Socialist German Workers Party (the Nazi Party), had gained control of government.

The Third Reich (1933–1945)

Just how much popular support the Nazis and their ideology actually received from the German populace is still a matter of controversy and emotional debate. What is beyond doubt is that the majority of Germans were thoroughly fed up with the violent class and political warfare combined with the economic hardship and instability that had been tearing Germany apart since 1918. They desperately wanted political and economic stability and security. For many, the Nazis seemed to offer just that. The Nazi policy of economic modernization, although based on creating a war machine, provided work for the unemployed as well as food and housing for those in need.

Their centralized ideology and message of social unity, while based on racial supremacist theories,[3] provided a social glue that seemed to help the country pull itself back together after the divisive clashes and violence of the previous twenty years. Just as the United States went through an identity crisis and period of self-criticism after the Vietnam War, Germany was radically divided by debate about the causes and blame for the loss of World War I. The Nazis spread rumors of a "stab in the back," blaming the loss on those Germans with more democratic and socialist leanings, in particular those who were then governing Weimar Germany. In fact, the first concentration camps were built by the Nazis to house those German socialists, union leaders, and communists who were branded as traitors for their attempts to create a more egalitarian society.

The Nazi carrot-and-stick tactic of creating jobs, solving

housing and food shortages, and fostering a new German identity that restored lost pride on the one hand while institutionalizing political repression and terror tactics to punish and intimidate dissidents on the other was successful in rapidly establishing complete political control over the country. How many of the Nazi leaders' ultimate goals and strategies—for example, the "Final Solution"—were known by the populace at large is an open question. Without doubt, antisemitism had a long and ugly history in Germany, as it did in most European countries. But in the early years of their regime, the Nazis concentrated more on reviving Germany's economic and military power, while working feverishly to gain complete political control. In its later stages, the dictatorship had gained so much power that few could challenge it. And once World War II actually began, the patriotism of most Germans inclined them to work for victory and to ignore all else. It will probably never be possible to fully determine what percentage of the populace was truly loyal to the party's ideology, how many were simply opportunistic, and how many went along for fear of also ending up in the camps.

For those Americans who might believe that there is something unique about the Germans or their personalities that brought the Nazi experience upon them, it is wise to remember that as experimental research by social scientists in the United States has shown,[4] even average Americans are susceptible to becoming sadistic and blindly obedient to authority when their social roles and external conditions demand it.

I mean in no way to pardon or excuse the horrors and barbarities that occurred under the Nazi regime. Like other attempts at genocide, these must rank as unholy blemishes on human history. However, we must at the same time recognize the realities of the human condition and more clearly understand that cultural, political, and situational factors—not some inborn genetic programming—more fully explain these terrible events. Only by understanding that "German" is not synonymous with "Nazi" can we move past our stereotypical thinking and learn to communicate openly and effectively with Germans.

Der Zusammenbruch (1945–1949)

Germans refer to 1945 as the *Stunde Null* (zero hour), and the period after the war is known as the *Zusammenbruch*, or collapse. While the majority of the world joyously celebrated the end of the war, for ordinary German citizens, this period was more difficult than the war itself. Fearing ethnic cleansing and the advancing Soviet armies, millions of expellees and refugees from the east flooded into western Germany. These additional people overburdened a country where food and shelter were already scarce. Hunger and malnutrition were constant problems. It is estimated that the average citizen subsisted on fewer than eight hundred calories per day. Like its cities, the country's economic and political infrastructure also lay in ruins. From 1945 through June of 1948, German currency was basically worthless, and barter and the black market were the major sources of food and other consumer goods, which created an atmosphere of crime, lawlessness, guilt, and shame that intensified the trauma brought on by the loss of the war and the death of so many friends, relatives, and loved ones.

Because the end of the war marked the beginning of a transition to the Cold War, Germany was divided into four zones of occupation, with the Soviets in the eastern zones and the Americans, British, and French in the western zones. These divisions were never meant to be permanent, but as the Cold War progressed, the lines hardened into the boundaries that would later become East and West Germany.

German Democratic Republic (1949–1990)

The German Democratic Republic (GDR), or East Germany, was founded in the Soviet zone in response to the creation of the Federal Republic of Germany in the western zones of occupation. The GDR became part of the Soviet bloc and was governed by a communist party along the lines of the Soviet model. Its centralized, state-run economy became the strongest in the communist economic bloc, providing the East Germans with the basics of life, if not with the great variety and quality of consumer goods those in the western zones enjoyed.

Germans in the GDR seemed less disturbed by the lack of material abundance and lower-quality consumer goods than they were about the lack of media freedom and their inability to travel. After the founding of the GDR, there was still no actual barrier between East and West Germany. It was only in 1961, with the building of the Berlin Wall to stop the steady migration of East Germans to the western zones, that the East Germans were suddenly denied access to their friends and relatives in West Germany.

But while the economy of the GDR seemed strong because of its position in the communist system, in fact it was much weaker than even the experts had guessed. Many industries had survived only because of heavy subsidies. Crucial investments in infrastructure, new plants, and more modern technologies had not been made because of the lack of hard currency. As glasnost and perestroika in Russia spread through the Eastern bloc, the GDR found itself in an untenable political position. By 1989 the regime was toppled by a peaceful revolution, the first in German history. In 1990, those orphans of the Cold War, East and West Germany, were finally reunited.

Federal Republic of Germany (1949–1968)

After World War II, the so-called "German Question" again occupied the minds of the world's political leaders. What was to be done with a nation that had already risen phoenixlike from the ashes of one world war only to start a second? Should it be completely deindustrialized and made an agrarian country as some proposed, or was there a better solution?

As in the forming of East Germany, the events of the Cold War played a major role in the decision in 1949 to form the *Bundesrepublik Deutschland* (BRD), or as we call it in English, the Federal Republic of Germany (FRG), in the zones occupied by the Americans, British, and French. Shortly prior to the actual founding of the FRG, a currency reform was initiated by the German government with the help of the three occupying powers. By now the Cold War was intensifying, and the countries of the West wanted assurance that West Germany would serve as a bulwark against the expansion of Soviet communism. They hoped that by allowing Germany to rebuild they could not only staunch the flow of communism but also create an economically healthy and politically democratic West Germany that would not be susceptible to the rise of radical parties as had occurred after World War I. To date, this strategy has functioned as hoped.

The economic recovery of Germany was nothing less than astounding. The aid granted by the Marshall Plan played a critical role, but it was the discipline, determination, and industrial flair of the Germans that helped create this recovery, which is referred to as the *Wirtschaftswunder* (economic miracle). By the end of the 1950s German industry was again a force to be reckoned with in the world. This creation of a vibrant industrial economy has had several major repercussions for the FRG.

First, with the rapid growth of industry, large numbers of workers were needed in the plants and factories. Because so many men had died during the war, the German government looked outside its borders for help. Large numbers of workers from Turkey, Italy, Greece, Yugoslavia, and Spain began arriving in Germany to fill the vacancies. Prior to 1945 there had been very little geographic or social mobility within the country. Because they lived in a class society, Germans were used to having little contact with persons from other classes or occupations. And because most people lived in the same town or region as their ancestors had, they possessed a strong, centuries-old provincialism and sense of tradition. Strangers were viewed with suspicion, as were new ways of doing things. The influx of *Gastarbeiter* (guest workers) combined with the large numbers of ethnic German refugees who had already arrived from the east upset the previous cultural and ethnic stability of Germany.

While the ethnic German refugees were assimilated fairly easily, the guest workers, with their southern Mediterranean and Turkish cultures, were not, an issue that is examined later in chapter 7.

Federal Republic of Germany (1968–1990)

If the late 1940s and 1950s were years of struggling out from under the rubble in order to rebuild a modern society, the 1960s saw the material results of that struggle. Germany's infrastructure had been rebuilt, and the economy was becoming one of the most powerful in the world, creating an affluent society that most Germans had never known before.

By the 1960s a generation was growing up that had watched their parents struggle to rebuild their country, but who had rarely had the time or wherewithal to talk about how that destruction had come to be. Most of the *Nachkriegsgeneration* (postwar generation) had worked with great industry and unswerving perseverance to rebuild Germany economically and politically, but in so doing they had basically swept the issue of the Nazis and the war under the carpet. Only artists, writers, intellectuals, and a few political leaders took issue with Germany's Nazi past.

The younger generation chose a different approach. The late 1960s was a time of radical social change throughout most of the Western world. Protests against the war in Vietnam were not limited to the United States but occurred throughout Europe as well. Social justice and emancipation were common themes on the lips of many people. In Germany this social movement took aim at a special target: Germany's most recent history.

Following the lead of an intellectual avant-garde, university students and some instructors began examining the Nazi era as part of what has come to be called *Vergangenheitsbewältigung* (coming to terms with the past). One of the most commonly asked questions was how a civilized country such as Germany could fall prey to the barbarities of the Nazis. For many of the younger Germans this question took on a more personal form: what did my parents do during the war and why did they not resist? These questions were first asked at universities, but their shock waves soon spread to the rest of society.

Spurred on by intellectual and political leaders, many students spent long hours confronting their country's past, both in private and in the classroom. These talks fit in with the spirit of the times and led to massive political demonstrations, which forced the subject into living rooms across the country, where it was heatedly debated. As the younger Germans posed that fateful question to their parents—"What did you do during the war?"—Germany became embroiled in a national discussion that continues to the present day. The amazing debate in the *Bundestag* (German parliament) in the spring of 1997 about the role of the German army during World War II is only one facet of this continuing discussion.[5]

By opening this subject for public discussion, the student movement created a huge generation gap, which still exists. Those young Germans who were politically active during this time and who identified with the student movement are often referred to as the "Generation of '68." The strong German peace movement, which had existed since the beginning of the FRG, was strengthened, and seeds were planted for the environmental movement, which led to the founding of the Green Party. Out of this rebellious period also grew the left-wing terrorist movement (Baader-Meinhof Group, Red Army Faction), who engaged in violent attacks on the establishment.

As a result of this period of political and social activism, German life has changed in many ways. Two of the most important changes relate to education and child raising. While a clearly democratic political framework had been created for the FRG in 1949, many older Germans were still imbued with the traditional attitudes and behaviors left over from their authoritarian past. In order to understand the successful rise to power of the Nazis, sociologists critically examined the traditional German class structure, and psychologists applied their concept of the "authoritarian personality." While no definitive answer emerged, what did become clear was that having a rigid class structure and raising children to obey all authority were major factors in the Nazi takeover. Many Germans became convinced that radical changes in educational structures and child-raising practices would be the best antidote to prevent a resurgence of fascism.

In the early 1970s agitation began for a new educational system that would be more democratic and available to members of all classes. As a result, educational reforms were enacted which opened the previously elitist school system to more children from the working classes. Because of these changes, 37.5 percent of German children completed the *Abitur* (academic school-leaving exam) in 1995, compared with about 10 percent in 1970.[6] Because the Abitur is also the entry ticket to a German university, proportionately more young Germans now have a college education than ever before. This democratization of the educational system has been a subject of intense analysis and debate since these reforms were put in place.

In addition, many of the Generation of '68 chose to raise their children in what they claimed was an antiauthoritarian manner. Children were to be given the opportunity to grow up "freer," without being forcibly pressed into following what were considered outdated or unreasonable social conventions. Much of traditional German life was called into question by the Generation of '68, and their children were raised without the excessive demands for respect and obedience that had characterized child raising in the past. Opinions about the validity of the antiauthoritarian upbringing are many and still serve as a point of emotional debate for Germans. Regardless of ideological viewpoint, most Germans agree that younger generations today differ from older, more traditional Germans in a number of important ways. It is fair to say that they are generally less nationalistic, more democratic, and better informed than previous generations.

In the course of openly discussing their country's recent past, these same students also confronted the older generations with their questions and accusations. This set off wave after wave of self-examination and self-criticism in the FRG. No other example comes to mind that compares with Germany's willingness to look so closely at the mistakes of its past in such an open and objective way. Much of the credit for this remarkable feat goes to the younger generation of Germans. Equally important, they have attempted to change the way they communicate, cultivating a more open, less authoritarian style of speech. See the section on *du* and *Sie* in chapter 4 for an example of the kinds of changes that have occurred in communication.

How much these changes tore apart the German social fabric is illustrated by the following incident. In 1987 I was returning to Germany after a long vacation in the United States. A friend picked me up at the airport in Stuttgart. After collecting my luggage, we went to her car to find the following message written in the dust on the hood: *Der Zustand des Autos läßt auf den Zustand Ihres Geistes schließen* (The condition of your car says a lot about the condition of your mind). We were both brought up short. Admittedly, my friend was a member of the younger generation with leftist leanings, and she did sometimes go out of her way to behave in a manner that was designed to provoke the more traditional bourgeois Germans. That the car hadn't been washed or cleaned up in quite a while was pretty obvious, but that someone would be so offended by the car as to take the time to express his or her moral indignation in this manner struck me as exaggerated. The tone was angrily indignant and not at all humorous like the simple "wash me" phrase sometimes written on dusty American cars and trucks. Clearly, an older, more conservative German saw this dirty car as an affront to public order and felt compelled to express his or her irritation. Equally incensed, my young friend was angry and disturbed that "these damned fascists are still active." As the next chapter will show, order and cleanliness are dear to the traditional German heart, and because of this, those traits were direct targets for the students and activists of the 1960s.

While the late 1960s and early 1970s were a time of intense political activity and great change in Germany, that intensity had eased up somewhat by the late 1970s. To be sure, the peace movement, the founding of the Green Party, the antinuclear protests, and the periods of economic slump continued to provide the Germans with reasons for concern. Nevertheless, the next major wave in the series of dramatic changes occurred with the reunification of East and West Germany.

Reunification (1990–Present)

Poland's Solidarity movement and Gorbachev's promotion of glasnost and perestroika in the Soviet Union set the stage for the liberation movements that took place in most of the Eastern bloc countries. The period of peaceful revolution in the GDR was called *die Wende* (the change or turning point) and lasted from the autumn of 1989 until the first free elections in March of 1990. Die Wende was preceded in the summer of 1989 by an increasing—legal and illegal—exodus of GDR citizens, which put great pressure on both the East and West German governments. Pressure in East Germany increased in the autumn, when large street protests began occurring, first in Leipzig and then elsewhere.

Seeing that noncommunist governments had been set up in Poland and Hungary without Soviet reprisals, the East German protest movement became bolder. The government, headed by Erich Honecker, seemed powerless to prevent the demonstrations, which were growing in size and frequency. Even within the GDR's Communist Party, many were demanding change, and on October 18 Honecker was forced to resign. Realizing that change was imminent, his replacement, Egon Krenz, opened negotiations with church leaders and intellectuals who led up the protest movement. This accelerated the pace of change. Then, on November 9 a most unimaginable and spectacular event occurred: the GDR announced its citizens were now free to travel across any of the border checkpoints, in effect tearing a giant hole in the Berlin Wall. That night thousands of East Berliners poured into West Berlin for a joyous celebration of reunion with their cousins from the west. It was a moment of undreamed-of euphoria for these people who had chafed so long at the travel restrictions imposed on them.

The demonstrations for reform gained in size and success, but while the original dissident intellectuals and leaders had hoped for reforms and changes in the socialist system, the masses, who joined the movement in ever-increasing numbers, wanted not reform but complete dissolution of the GDR and reunification with the FRG. They wanted a Western lifestyle quickly and showed no interest in preserving the advantages of the GDR's system. They voted in great numbers with their feet—many young East Germans left for West Germany, where they were constitutionally guaranteed West German citizenship. Their large numbers were a destabilizing factor for the West German society and economy, putting strong pressure on the West German government. When Helmut Kohl, chancellor of West Germany, visited the GDR in December of 1989, his proposal for reunification was widely cheered by the East Germans.

The government of the GDR finally conceded, and free elections took place on March 18, 1990. The clear victory of the Christian Democratic Union (CDU) was an unambiguous mandate for reunification, and plans proceeded rapidly.

The two Germanys were formally reunited at midnight on October 2, 1990. It was another moment of euphoria, but as time would show, this euphoria was premature. The reunification was an untried experiment on a huge scale, and no one was sure how it would proceed. Chancellor Kohl had made promises of no increased taxes for the west and a painless integration of the two countries, promises that were soon shown to be untenable. Disappointment set in rapidly on both sides.

German reunification can in fact be said to have experienced three chronological phases to date. The first phase, like a honeymoon, was marked by euphoria and joyous celebration of the new relationship, as just mentioned. Unfortunately, though, like many honeymoons, it was brief in duration, leading into a second phase marked by bitter disappointment. If the first phase was characterized by an attitude of "Hurrah, the Wall is finally down," the slogan of the second phase would have been, "Let's put the Wall back up and make it higher."

After the establishment of the German monetary union between East and West Germany in July of 1990, Western goods began appearing in East German shops. But then a plethora of problems emerged that had not been anticipated in the initial excitement. The first was that the East German economy was far weaker than had been thought. Many plants were hopelessly antiquated, the infrastructure was inadequate, pollution was horrendous, and questions regarding ownership of property were complicated. All of these problems made foreign investors wary, which resulted in plant closings, and many East Germans soon found themselves unemployed.

As unemployment increased, so too did rents and the price of food and other goods. The East Germans had never had access to a wide assortment of consumer goods or foods, but under the communist regime they had at least had the basic necessities of life and guaranteed employment. As unemployment skyrocketed and the government of the FRG imposed itself on the east, the initial euphoria began to dissipate. Confusion and conflicting emotions became commonplace among East Germans, and many wondered if reunification hadn't been a mistake.

They complained about the lack of solidarity, the competitive and arrogant attitudes of the *Wessis* (West Germans), and the harshness of the western system. Many *Ossis* (East Germans) thought back nostalgically to the job security, the lower rents and food prices, the slower pace of life, and the group solidarity and other advantages they had enjoyed before reunification. This was a time of great soul-searching. Anger, bewilderment, and self-pity were common, especially among older East Germans, who believed they would not be able to adapt to these newer ways and who felt their lives had largely been wasted. Younger East Germans were more able to take the changes in stride, but the period since the Wende has been one of great trauma for many former East German citizens.

It is difficult for an outsider to imagine the magnitude of the social upheaval in this vast experiment. When the citizens of the GDR voted to join West Germany, few knew what they were getting into. Remodeling the former GDR along the lines of West Germany meant that the east took on a brand-new constitution, complete with a new legal and administrative system. Not only were the East Germans unfamiliar with how this legal and administrative system worked, the only people with any administrative and legal experience were the former communists, and no one wanted them back in power. This meant that large numbers of experts from former West Germany had to come east to help out, adding more insult to the East Germans' already injured pride. Similarly, the educational system needed new teachers and textbooks, and the press and media also had to be westernized. All of these changes were more complex and took far more time and money than anyone had expected. Combined with the problems of unemployment and soaring expenses, they created a very difficult social and political atmosphere throughout Germany.

Now, nine years since the Wende, great progress has been made to integrate the two Germanys, but much still remains to be done. Germany can now be said to be in the third phase of reunification: adaptation and accommodation. Both the initial euphoria and following disappointment are being replaced by more open-minded and realistic attitudes. And the differences that exist between east and west have not disappeared. In fact they will probably remain for generations to come, as have other regional differences in the FRG.

Germany: A Patchwork Country

The differences between East and West Germans are only one example of important regional variations among the Germans. Recall that Germany in the Middle Ages had been a patchwork of small independent kingdoms, duchies, principalities, and free cities until united under Prussian dominance in 1871. Each of these small entities had been an independent state with its own monetary, legal, tax, educational, and political systems, and while much of this variety has been smoothed over by the creation of a centralized federal government and through the influence of the mass media, great variation still exists in customs, behaviors, and dialects as well as in attitudes and philosophy.

The patchwork nature of Germany is attributable to a complex interaction of many factors, such as the already-mentioned Germanic custom of dividing a man's inheritance equally among his sons. Geography also played a role: the lack of rapid transportation and heavily forested terrain served to hinder cross-border commerce and traffic between the various regions. More importantly, what was to become Germany was surrounded by stronger, more centralized empires, in particular France and Austria, who played the smaller German states off against each other to keep them weak and unorganized.

One useful result of Germany's fragmented past is that today Germany is a polycentric federation. Many of the current federal states are direct outgrowths of the former Germanic kingdoms and principalities. Unlike France, Spain, and Britain, with their historically centralized systems revolving around one major capital city, Germany exists as a series of smaller, interlinked centers, each of which had at one time been the capital of a smaller kingdom. There is no one megalopolis that completely dominates German politics, economy, and culture as do Paris and London; rather, each large city is a small, autonomous center in its own right. And although Berlin is once again the official capital, Munich, Frankfurt, Stuttgart, Hamburg, Leipzig, and other smaller cities remain important economic, political, and cultural centers. Additionally, regional governments throughout Germany remain major players in German politics—all of which is reinforced by the structure of the German parliament, the upper house of which is composed of directly appointed representatives from the state governments.

One of the most positive results of this lack of centralization is the German public transport system. Unlike a spider's web which radiates out in all directions from a single central city, as in France, Germany's system is a coordinated matrix, making travel faster and more convenient while contributing significantly to Germany's economic strength.

While Frankfurt—particularly in its role as headquarters for the European Union's central bank—will continue to be Germany's financial center and the site of its principal stock market, the regional stock markets will continue to play a significant role. Many thought these smaller markets should be consolidated with Frankfurt, but now it seems some will become specialty markets, filling in niches not covered by the Frankfurt Center.

Another example of Germany's regional diversity is seen in the many towns and cities, each with its own well-financed symphonies, theaters, operas, museums, and arts programs. Germany is a less popularistic culture than the United States, and such cultural institutions are viewed by the general public as important and worthy of support with public monies.

Nor is this diversity confined only to infrastructure and culture. Perhaps nowhere is it so clearly visible as in the number of independent breweries spread across this small country. Despite major national advertising campaigns and some consolidations of breweries, few beers do well throughout the entire German market. Instead, there are thousands of excellent local brews that have a loyal following among the inhabitants of the regions.

Germans are intensely loyal to their *Heimat*, the local area where they were born and raised. Unlike Americans, who are known for their willingness to pick up and move when an economic opportunity presents itself, Germans have traditionally been far less willing to leave their local region. While this has changed in the last few years, especially as more students have gone off to college in other areas, most still cling tightly to their regional roots. Because of the stigma attached to Germany's past, many citizens tend to place more importance on their regional than their national identity. One person from the south of Germany (Bavarians are especially well known for their regional loyalty) declared, "I am Bavarian first, European second, and German third."

Regional identification is also particularly noticeable in the numerous German dialects still spoken. There have been some moves to abolish dialects in the schools, and some linguists have predicted that all dialects will die out in time. Nevertheless, they are currently alive and well, especially in the south. In fact, in some regions they are even regaining prestige previously lost to standard German. This linguistic diversity is remarkable in such a small country. While there are a variety of regional accents in the United States, they cannot compare to the number of dialects in Germany. Some of the dialects are even mutually exclusive; many Germans would not be able to understand one another if each were speaking only in his or her own dialect. For this reason, most speakers of a dialect have learned a toned-down dialect that resembles standard, or high, German (*Hochdeutsch*).

At the risk of offending some Germans, I offer the following generalization as a starting point for Americans trying to understand Germans: regional and dialect differences in Germany are most noticeable in the lower and lower-middle classes. As one climbs the social ladder, these variations generally play a lesser role, and educated Germans throughout the country are more similar in their attitudes, behaviors, and speech patterns than are those Germans who are less well educated. As is true in any nation, education tends to weaken provincialism as well as the traditions associated with particular regions. And, generally speaking, fewer people speak a dialect in the northern parts of Germany than in the south. The reasons for this are fascinating, complex, and well worth exploring if you are linguistically inclined.[7]

North-South Axis

North-south differences are noticeable in Germany, partly because they correlate positively with variations in religion as well as language use. Northern and eastern Germany are traditionally influenced by Protestant thought, while the south and west tend to be more Catholic. One telling illustration of the contrast in religious influences can be seen in the pre-Lent celebrations of *Fasching* and *Karneval*. These celebrations parallel Mardi Gras in New Orleans or Carnival in Rio and are marked by days of raucous parties and large, colorful parades. While the predominantly Protestant regions go about their normal daily routines during this time, the Catholic sections of the country celebrate on a grand scale. Their dissimilar approach to this time of year is reflective of the two religions and the differences in their attitude toward life. The Protestants tend to take a more serious view of life, whereas the Catholics view life more as a source of enjoyment. But saying that northerners are more reserved, more likely to be Protestant, and less likely to speak a dialect is simplistic. The pattern of regional differences is far more complex than this. For example, specific smaller regions are the sources of many stereotypes regarding particular personality traits. Thus, Rheinlanders are thought to talk more and are considered more cheerful and extroverted than the dour, serious, Protestant Swabians, who are famed for their thrift and industry. Many Germans explain this by citing the Catholic influence in the Rheinland and the Pietistic influence in Swabia. In fact, leading European sociologist Max Weber, in his landmark work, *The Protestant Ethic and the Spirit of Capitalism*, has shown how Protestant influences directly shaped economic development in different areas of Europe.[8]

Perhaps no region's stereotypes are more widely recognized or more often caricatured than those of Bavaria. The Bavarians are known for their *Gemütlichkeit* (sense of coziness, warmth, or intimacy) and open, friendly manner. It is generally agreed that Bavarians are quicker to use the familiar form of address and first names than are other Germans. In contrast, it is also widely agreed that people in the north talk faster, have fewer and shorter pauses in their speech, and are more emotionally reserved in personal relationships, warming up only slowly, and certainly not when they meet someone for the first time. For the northern German, the Bavarian's switch to first names is far too impulsive, too intrusive, and quite impolite. Northerners are more cautious in their interactions, preferring to get to know one another well before moving to a first-name basis, if they do so at all.

Just as knowing whether a German is from the north or south will give you some insight into his or her behavior, so will determining whether he or she is from the west or the east.

Differences between East and West

Detailing the differences between East and West Germans is difficult because not only did the forty-plus years of communist rule leave its mark, but also regional differences had existed in the east prior to the takeover. This again was the result of Germany's patchwork past. The Saxons, for instance, are thought of as more lively, humorous, temperamental, and easygoing than their direct neighbors, the severe and serious Prussians.

But in addition to these traditional differences, communism left an indelible mark on the East Germans. While certain personality traits and social behaviors were rewarded, others were marginalized. This is especially true for those older Germans who have lived most of their lives under communist influence. These Germans tend to be more group oriented, exhibiting a strong sense of solidarity and willingness to protect and help one another, which served as a survival function under the communists. These older Germans are less concerned about individual achievement than their West German cousins and are less competitive in the workplace. Instead, they tend to be more modest, more sociable, and more helpful toward their colleagues. Unlike West Germans, who strictly separate their business and personal lives, East Germans socialize more with their coworkers. Many of these traits are already changing significantly among the younger Germans in the east, resulting in a definite generation gap.

Another important distinction between east and west, especially for Americans, is that fewer East Germans speak English. Unlike West Germans, they were taught Russian rather than English at school. While the school curriculum has changed since reunification, it will be some years before English skill levels in the east match those in the west.

Another significant difference between the east and west is the approach taken toward Vergangenheitsbewältigung, or coming to terms with the past. Many younger West Germans know a great deal about their country's Nazi past and can talk about the subject fairly objectively. While the issue can still generate controversy and emotional debate, at least it is out of the closet and open for discussion. In the east the situation is different.

Because the Nazis viewed communists as their most dangerous political opponents, German communists and socialists were the first to suffer under Nazi persecution. When the GDR became a communist country, the leaders quickly distanced themselves from Germany's Nazi past. They declared that the Nazis were a product of capitalism and that it was the socialists who had fought the Nazis. In the leaders' opinion, it was absurd for them to take any responsibility for Nazi atrocities. Thus, while the GDR did more to get former Nazis out of jobs and positions of power than did the FRG, they also allowed their children to grow up with no sense of collective guilt for Germany's past. Today, these differences in attitude between East and West Germans toward their country's fascist history are gradually fading as democracy takes root throughout the country. Although the past will continue to be an issue that will occupy all Germans, east and west, for years to come, regional differences in this regard can be expected to decrease. West and East Germans are getting to know one another better, and many of their negative stereotypes are being revised or set aside entirely.

Rural-Urban Variation

In addition to regional differences, rural and urban distinctions contribute a further, major source of variation within Germany. As in all parts of the world, the more traditional patterns of a culture can almost always be found in rural areas, and the same is true for Germany. In the countless small country towns and villages one finds older customs and more traditional patterns of behavior than in the urban areas. The same goes for ethnic homogeneity and dialects, both of which are more pronounced in the country than in the city. And it is there that Germany's agrarian past is still quite vibrantly alive in folk music, arts and crafts, and folk celebrations. Typically, the smaller towns and villages in the countryside are not subject to the more diverse social and cultural trends found in the cities.

In the cities there is a wealth of cultural diversity, especially in Frankfurt and Berlin. Because major German industry is principally located in the larger cities and urban areas, many immigrants and guest workers live and work in these centers. For example, Kreuzberg, an area of Berlin, was for a time inhabited predominantly by Turks. While this is changing, more Turks live in Berlin than in most Turkish cities. And in Frankfurt approximately 30 percent of the population is not ethnically German.

Given the significant differences between (1) the cities and rural areas and among the various regions; (2) ethnic, generational, and gender diversity; and (3) class distinctions and variations in educational background, valid generalizations about German culture are difficult to make. But one entry point into this highly complex pattern is the central values and norms that have helped give the Germans a sense of commonality and tradition.

---

[1] For an examination of how this historical approach influenced social scientists in the United States, see the Hardt article listed in the References.

[2] In June of 1922 one U.S. dollar was worth 350 marks; by November of 1923 the cost of a dollar was 4,200,000,000 marks.

[3] While it is natural for Americans to want to distance themselves emotionally and intellectually from the policies of the Nazis, there are some striking parallels in our own history. The theories of genetics on which the Nazis based their racial ideology were not all that different from the theories of eugenics popular in the United States and other European countries at that time. In the U.S. this theory was used to support and justify racism and segregation as well as the involuntary sterilization of minority women.

[4] After World War II, social scientists in the United States tried to understand what made so many Germans go along with the

sadistic and hateful policies of the Nazis. Stimulated by Adolph Eichmann's trial in Jerusalem for war crimes committed under the Nazi dictatorship, Stanley Milgram set out to find an answer through experimentation. The question Milgram asked was "Can a normal human being commit such atrocities?" Milgram and other American social scientists were shocked to discover the degree to which ordinary Americans were willing to punish their fellow citizens with potentially fatal electric shocks when an authority figure ordered them to do so.

At a later date, social scientist Philip Zimbardo designed another experiment to answer the question "What effect does a prison have on the behavior of both the guards and the prisoners?" He set up a simulated prison using normal American college students as "guards" and "prisoners." Like Milgram, Zimbardo was shaken to discover the quick changes that occurred in the behavior of both the guards, who became sadistic, and the prisoners, who became excessively submissive as well as showing signs of significant emotional disturbance. The radical and unexpected changes in behavior occurred so quickly that the experiment had to be prematurely terminated. The conclusion was clear: it was much more the social context and role that one played and less one's personality that determine major dimensions of human behavior. For more information see Milgram or Haney and Zimbardo in the References.

5 I know of no example of a public political debate which was marked by such sincere, open, and authentic personal emotion by members of the various political factions. For more details see "Dieser Krieg läßt uns alle nicht los," *Die Zeit*, 13, 28 March 1997, 16.

6 "Vorwärts in der Vergangenheit," *Der Spiegel*, 23, 1995, 72–82.

7 For more on this fascinating subject, refer to Clyne or Barbour and Stevenson in the References.

8 Max Weber, *The Protestant Ethic and the Spirit of Capitalism* (London: George Allen & Unwin, 1976).

3

Major German Cultural Themes

In order to communicate successfully with people from other cultures, it is important to understand how they interpret a given situation and what their intentions are. To do this we must have some sense of their values, norms, and beliefs, which interact in a complex way to influence all behavior and communication. For the purpose of brevity I will call these complex interactions "cultural themes," because they run through a culture as a theme does through a book or a piece of music. Only when you understand the central cultural themes of any given culture can you accurately interpret and understand its inhabitants' behavior, communication, and way of life. If you don't understand their cultural themes, you will necessarily project your own values, norms, and beliefs onto them, and this projection is one of the principal causes of intercultural misunderstanding. If, however, you begin to learn the cultural themes, what before had seemed illogical or wrong behavior will take on a different meaning.

This chapter offers insights into seven central German cultural themes in an attempt to explain Germans' behavior and their way of life. By understanding how Germans understand the world, you will increase your chances of communicating more successfully with them.

Ordnung Muß Sein

Ordnung muß sein (there must be order) is a well-known and commonly heard saying in Germany; indeed one of the first things that strike visitors to Germany is its cleanliness and orderliness. Ordnung is a theme that permeates German society. Go into a German house and it will be very clean, with everything in its proper place. Walk into a mechanic's garage or carpenter's workshop and the tools and equipment will be well maintained and stored neatly. In German offices you will notice large numbers of well-kept files and special notebooks that are referred to as *Ordner*. The old saying "a place for everything and everything in its place" might well have originated in Germany. It is certainly a premise on which Germans like to operate.

The desire for Ordnung is also related to Germans' strict adherence to schedules and deadlines. Punctuality is a virtue, and lateness is seen as sloppiness or a sign of disrespect. Being late upsets the general Ordnung. Perhaps the country's railways offer the best illustration of German punctuality. The trains of the German railway system are famous for their punctuality. It is a standard joke that you can set your watch by a train's arrival and departure times. Germany has one of the world's best public transportation systems, and a major part of its success stems from the German sense of Ordnung. This system, which links almost every village, town, and city in Germany, is a striking example of the German ability to effectively organize and coordinate complex processes. Like the transportation system, the rest of the country's infrastructure is also well organized for the same reason.

One visible result of this well-regulated society is the condition of German autos. As the short anecdote in chapter 2 illustrated, Germans take their cars very seriously indeed. It is rare to see a car in Germany that is not well kept and in excellent mechanical condition. Germans take good care of all their property, but their cars are especially important because, more so than in the United States, they are a status symbol as well as a means of transportation. The fact that they are in such good mechanical condition is in large part due to the *Technischer Überwachungsverein*, or *TÜV*. This agency inspects all vehicles licensed in the country and is well known for the rigor with which its inspectors go about their job. A horn that doesn't work, broken turn signals, or rust in a crucial spot are all reasons for a car to fail this strict inspection. Inspections at a TÜV center are a microcosm of German orderliness. These inspection stations are spic-and-span, brightly lit, and operated by inspectors whose uniforms would be clean enough to be seen in a doctor's office. While administrators take care of the paperwork in a brisk, matter-of-fact way, the cars move through a series of checkpoints, where they are thoroughly inspected. I can well remember the feeling of apprehension in my stomach as I watched an inspector walking underneath my elevated car with a bright light and very large screwdriver. He was intent on finding any spot where rust might have weakened the car, and he did this by thrusting the screwdriver with resounding force into each and every section of the chassis and underbody. Luckily for me, all rusted areas had been fixed by welding heavy sheets of metal over them, or my car would have been one of the many that the TÜV pulled out of circulation.

Germans claim such rigor is necessary because of the large number of autos, especially on the Autobahn, where there is often no speed limit and where they put their vehicles through their paces. This can be unnerving to Americans not used to aggressive drivers who often come racing up from behind at over 120 miles per hour while blinking their headlights to warn you out of their way. And as might be expected, German drivers know each and every traffic rule and regulation by heart—the result of strict licensing exams and extensive and mandatory driver education programs typically costing more than $1,000—and they expect you to do the same. Forewarned is forearmed: defensive driving is still a foreign concept in Germany.

Ordnung: Rules and Regulations

The sense of Ordnung is not limited only to the Germans' material domain, it also strongly influences their social world. Germany is a society structured by a large number of explicit rules and regulations. One of the first encounters foreign residents have with the regulatory nature of German society is the *Einwohnermeldeamt* (resident's registration office). All residents of Germany are required to register with their local Einwohnermeldeamt and to notify that office whenever they move or change their place of residence. German bureaucracy can be irritating or confusing, if not downright intimidating, especially when one is waiting in long lines, filling out innumerable forms, or dealing with unfriendly civil servants. The good news is that while it is time-consuming in the beginning, at least it generally works fairly well. Don't forget that Germany is one of the more densely populated countries in the world, and its bureaucracy helps keep everything running smoothly.

Travel to German villages or small towns and you will be struck by how picturesque they appear. All of the houses are of a similar style and they present a pretty sight: roofs are covered with similar tiles and the colors harmonize. This is generally no coincidence but rather the result of a housing code that goes into great detail about how a house may be designed, painted, and equipped. While such detailed regulations often seem too confining to most Americans, the Germans see it as a way of ensuring a society that is concerned not only with individual rights but also with the common good. As we will see later, this notion of the common good and the social contract is an important part of the German mindset.

The rules that regulate Germany extend far beyond the many official laws and requirements. Unwritten codes of manners and customs also structure German social life. Some of these are detailed and quite explicit. Others are less so and are simply things that "one doesn't do." For example, there is even a protocol for hostess gifts. Because Germans are very protective of their homes and private lives, being invited into someone's home for dinner is an honor. But once in-vited, there are many rules about how to behave.[1] For in-stance, it is customary to bring the hostess a bouquet of flowers. Germans love flowers and florist shops are abundant. But not just any flowers will do. Red roses symbolize ro-mance, so be careful to whom you give them. And white chrysanthemums and carnations are generally reserved for funerals. Also, it is proper to give bouquets consisting of an odd number of flowers. No one seems to really know why this custom is important. Some Germans say it's an old supersti-tion; others justify the custom by claiming an odd number makes for a more aesthetic arrangement.

Be that as it may, Germans feel comfortable with these kinds of rules, which give them a feeling of security as well as a strong sense of what is right and wrong. This sense of right and wrong is often expressed openly and emotionally by Germans, especially when they think someone has done some-thing wrong. This can seem overly judgmental or rude at times, but Germans prefer structure to an ambiguous situa-tion where no one seems to know the correct way to proceed.

At times it appears Germans have a rule for everything— and they do, almost! This is an aspect of what Germans call *Gründlichkeit*, or thoroughness. Germans are great believers in doing things thoroughly, and this has led to their reputa-tion as perfectionists. If they are going to do something, they spare little expense or time in doing it well. And if they can't do it thoroughly, they are inclined not to do it at all. As a German carpenter once told me, "If I don't have the time to do it right in the first place, when will I get the time to fix it later?" It is this logic which underlies the reputation Ger-many has for producing such high-quality automobiles and other products. Gründlichkeit is also an important compo-nent in the decision-making processes in traditional German organizations (see chapter 6) and is often a source of misun-derstanding in German and American joint ventures.

For Americans with their strong sense of individualism and belief in personal freedom, the German devotion to order can seem obsessive and highly constricting, even invasive, but there is little getting around the varied laws and regulations, because they are generally strictly enforced. At times they irritate the Germans, too. I remember the indignation of a German friend who had gotten a ticket for not locking her car when she parked it. When she complained to the police, she was told the rule was in place to discourage auto theft. German rules can all be rationally justified, and German officials will quickly do just that.

Ordnung: An Antidote for Anxiety

This respect for rational justification is crucial to understanding the concept of Ordnung and the German psyche. Germans have an extremely high regard for rational, analytic thought. Like most Protestant countries of northern Europe, Germany was strongly influenced by the ideas of the Enlightenment, the Age of Reason, with its emphasis on intellect, reason, and learning. Germany, Prussia in particular, was quick to adopt the notion of the rationally organized society. With this mindset in place, Prussia reorganized its army and created a strong bureaucracy, which contributed greatly to its military prowess. Prussia's success in defeating the French and finally uniting Germany convinced educated Germans of the effectiveness of organizing society based on rationalism.

The positive effects of rationality, however, explain only part of the Germans' strong desire for Ordnung. The opposite of Ordnung, chaos, is something which the typical German abhors. Chaos causes anxiety and insecurity and is a continual threat to order. Chaos occurs at many levels and can take many forms: social unrest, rising crime rates, economic malaise, unruly students, or any unresolved issue. Even dirty streets or an unwashed auto can be construed as evidence that chaos is ever-present and waiting to spring. This deep-rooted suspicion that chaos, or at least disorder, is lurking around every corner is a major cause of the angst and insecurity for which Germans are known.

The degree to which anxiety and insecurity influence German culture often puzzles foreign visitors. People everywhere in the world have to deal with unexpected setbacks, illnesses, and disasters that life presents, but Germans appear inordinately insecure and seem to worry much more than necessary about crises or emergencies that may never occur. Ordnung is one means by which Germans attempt to alleviate their insecurity. This worrying about the future often makes Germans seem gloomy and overly serious. It also makes them very risk-aversive, particularly when compared with Americans, many of whom thrive on risk taking. These fears and security needs are easier to understand in the context of Germany's turbulent history.

For centuries Germany has been a major battlefield for both civil and European wars, and this has left a deep mark on the German psyche. These wars brought with them chaos and suffering and destroyed the social and economic advances that Germans had worked so hard to achieve. Unemployment and inflation have also been the basis for German anxieties. In this century alone Germans have twice lost all their personal savings because of inflation and economic collapse brought about by war. This loss may explain the current German pride in their currency, the beloved *deutsche Mark* (DM), and their resistance to adopting the euro. Although the motive for their pride in the mark is not always conscious, it symbolizes the rebuilding of Germany and the stability and order which the economic miracle of the late 1950s and 1960s created.

Another major factor contributing to their desire for Ordnung is their distrust of the wild and romantic side of the German personality: the music, myths, and literature as well as the *Wanderlust* (desire to roam or travel) of the German people. When the Angles and Saxons left the continent for England, they took with them the epic poem *Beowulf*. This story tells of a great Germanic hero who, in his quest for fame and fortune, was required to dive into the dark depths of a large lake and seek out the lair of a hideous monster, the ferocious Grendel, who had ravaged the local people and whom no one could defeat. Perhaps no other tale so well symbolizes the romantic side of the German soul. It is a tale of adventure, heroism, and great camaraderie among Germanic warriors. It also symbolizes the depth of the German soul, which has given the world such wonderful art and music, but which is also at times a wild and seemingly uncontrollable beast, always ready to break out and wreak havoc and turmoil. Another example of this impulsive, irrational side of the Germans can be seen in the *Sturm und Drang* movement (Storm and Stress, 1767–1785), which was a passionately emotional reaction to the rationality of the Enlightenment as well as a forerunner to the Romantic movement, which shortly thereafter spread throughout Europe. Similarly, the music of Richard Wagner and Ludwig van Beethoven, the art of the German Expressionists, and the mythic approach to history taken by the Nazis are all manifestations of this wildly emotional side of the Germans. For centuries Germans, like other groups, have been trying to control this irrational side of their nature, and their idealization of Ordnung and rationality is, in part, an attempt to do so.

Ordnung: The Class System and Education

Traditionally the official German class system served as the prime creator of social Ordnung, structuring German social life until 1918, when it ended with the emperor's abdication. Before 1918 the three major classes—the aristocracy, the *Bürgertum* (professional and commercial middle class), and the lower class (workers and farmers)—lived in separate social worlds, their lives intersecting only tangentially. There were great discrepancies in wealth, lifestyle, and political power among these classes, and people tended to identify strongly with their own class, while looking with disdain or envy upon members of the other classes. Because of this, interactions between members of different classes were marked by reserve and mistrust and were very formal in nature.

While the class society was officially disbanded in 1918, its influence can still be found in German culture today. Certainly the German acceptance of hierarchy, social roles, and the importance of social status is directly related to the structure and mentality of the old class society. While the aristocracy no longer officially exists, social standing still plays a large role in people's behavior.

Perhaps the most obvious vestige of the old class society is the German school system, and here, too, Ordnung plays its part in the rigid tracking of students. During the first four years of schooling, all German children attend the *Grundschule* (basic school). After leaving the Grundschule, they go to one of three types of schools: *Gymnasium*, *Realschule*, or *Hauptschule*. The Gymnasium is the most academic of the three, requires the longest attendance, and is meant to prepare its pupils for entry into universities. The Realschule prepares its pupils for administrative and middle-management positions, while the Hauptschule provides a more vocational education for those who will later enter Germany's extensive apprenticeship program.

Traditionally, only children from the upper and middle classes attended the Gymnasium. Children from the working class were expected to attend the Hauptschule and then apprentice to one of the trades. Until the early 1970s the percentage of German children attending the Gymnasium was relatively low. Since then the number has risen steadily, while those graduating from the Hauptschule has fallen. By 1995 the number of graduates from the two types of school had become approximately the same.[2]

The importance of education in Germany can hardly be overestimated. Occupational success and social standing go hand in hand with educational qualifications. Most employers will not even consider someone for a job who does not have the proper education and credentials. In addition, for Germans, having a formal education means great respect as well as high status. In contrast with the United States, teachers are well paid and highly respected. And while businesspeople are often looked at skeptically, university professors enjoy higher prestige as well as generous salaries.

Having a university degree is often a prerequisite for group membership at higher social levels, and a preponderance of bonding and relationship building occurs while one is at the university. Because of the strong private-public distinction and the desire for tighter, more committed connections, middle- and upper-class Germans typically find it difficult to enter into close personal relationships later in life.

Finally, still other factors are involved in this idealization of Ordnung, including climate, religion, authoritarian upbringing, and a strong reliance on rational-analytic mental processes. Nor has this idealization of Ordnung remained constant. Germany has gone through radical economic and sociopolitical changes in this century and continues to do so. The process of change in values goes hand in hand with the more external socioeconomic changes—what the Germans call the *Wertewandel* (changing of values; see chapter 7). This has clearly had its influence on German ideas about Ordnung. While older Germans often seem obsessed with cleanliness, order, and rules, younger Germans are much more relaxed and flexible about them. These younger Germans know the horrors of their country's past, but they have also had the opportunity to grow up in an affluent and democratic society in which social norms have changed considerably. Families and schools are significantly less authoritarian than they were before the Wertewandel, and these changes have given the younger generation a more optimistic, easygoing outlook on life.

Insiders and Outsiders

Vestiges of the class system also play a part in the way Germans distinguish between "insiders" and "outsiders." Insiders are those persons who belong to the same group with which a German identifies. Depending on the situation, this could be the family, a group of friends, a social club, members of the same company, someone speaking the same regional dialect, and so on.

Germans distinguish clearly between insiders and outsiders on all levels. On the national level this distinction can be seen in Germany's citizenship policy. While many people from other ethnic groups have lived and worked in Germany for decades, the German government has done little to help them become citizens or to integrate them into German society. This often holds true even for their children, who were born and raised in Germany and who speak fluent German.

On the other hand, persons from Eastern European countries claiming ethnic German status—even if only through a German great-grandfather—have been granted entry and have easily obtained German citizenship, although in many cases they could barely speak German.

This is a sore spot for Germans and the subject of much debate. Clearly, xenophobia and racism are to be found in Germany, as elsewhere throughout the world. But what is telling about the German version is the country's official immigration and naturalization policy. While racism is evident in other countries such as France, Great Britain, and the United States, these countries make it much easier for aliens to gain citizenship. The clear distinction Germans draw between insiders and outsiders contributes to an official policy that makes nationalization difficult for non-Germans residing in Germany. However, as detailed in chapter 7, changes in this policy are slowly taking place.

On a less official level, the old German institution of the *Stammtisch* provides another example of the insider-outsider distinction. When you go into a German pub or restaurant, you will notice that no one leads you to a table. You are expected to choose your own table, and you can sit where you prefer. But you will generally find at least one table that is marked as the Stammtisch. If you try to sit at this table, even if no one else is sitting there, you will be politely informed that this is the Stammtisch, a special table reserved for regulars and that you must sit elsewhere. Such groups of regulars know each other well and meet frequently to play cards, gossip, or vigorously discuss everything under the sun.

When Germans are in a group with which they identify and there are no outsiders present, they talk about being *unter uns* (among ourselves). Being unter uns creates a sense of security and solidarity and directly influences the way Germans communicate. When outsiders are present, Germans are significantly more formal, more reserved, and less friendly. When only insiders are present, they open up and speak much more sincerely about topics they would never discuss with outsiders. As will be explored later, being an insider also brings with it commitment and obligation toward the other members of the group. This sense of internal solidarity and duty to the other members also makes it far more difficult for outsiders to enter the group. Americans, in contrast, try to facilitate the entry of new members to their group. For this reason, groups in the United States tend to be looser. They consist of less permanently connected networks of people and have more permeable boundaries.

For Americans accustomed to meeting strangers and being welcomed openly by them, the German formality and aloofness may seem cold and unfriendly. For Germans, on the other hand, it is being friendly toward strangers that is seen as unusual—and not necessarily positive. Whereas Americans often equate formality with unfriendliness and lack of ease, Germans have been raised to view reserve and formality as the proper signs of respect for people they don't know well. Because of this strong insider-outsider distinction, an insider's introduction can do wonders in facilitating your entry to German groups, whether they be social or work-related.

Clarity and Compartmentalization

Alles klar is another ubiquitous phrase in Germany and usually means "everything is okay." Translated literally, it means "all is clear," and *Klarheit* (clarity) is something Germans desire in most areas of their lives, from their relationships to their way of talking to their very thought processes. Like Ordnung, it is a constant theme that is interwoven in varying degrees through all levels of German culture. In their spatial orientation, a perfect example of clarity can be seen in the fences, gates, and walls that surround all German houses and yards. These fences clearly and exactly mark the boundaries between the different properties and serve as a protective wall, limiting entry from outside. Lawns and yards without clear boundaries, which inexactly blend into one another, like those found in many American towns and suburbs, are too ambiguous for Germans. They believe instead that Robert Frost's "Good fences make good neighbors" is actually more German than American. Given the limited space and high population density in Germany, this attitude makes sense.

Similarly, for guests invited into a German home, there are clear boundaries to be observed. Giving guests "a tour of the house," as often occurs in American homes, is rare in Germany. Americans often do this to show off their house and to create a relaxed, informal atmosphere so that their guests feel at home. Dinner guests in Germany rarely get to see the inside of the kitchen, let alone a tour that includes the bedrooms. Germans maintain a formal atmosphere by having the house perfectly neat and orderly, by spending much time preparing for their guests, and by using their best tablecloth, silverware, plates, and so on. The message they are sending is one of respect for such a special occasion as having a guest in their house.

The desire for clear borders also extends into Germans' interpersonal relationships. As they say, *Klare Rechnung, gute Freundschaft.* Literally this translates to "clear bill, good friendship," which means that when all crucial matters are made explicitly clear, then you can have a good friendship. Ideally, Germans view beating around the bush, vagueness of expression, and ambiguous definitions as major causes of misunderstandings and problems. This strong desire for clarity leads to a very direct and frank style of speaking, which is sometimes overly direct and blunt for non-German sensibilities. It also often leads Germans to overlook the feelings of the person they are talking with in order to be direct and honest. As the next chapter will show, this desire for clarity and the corresponding directness in speech are a crucial part of the German communication style.

The mutual influences of clarity and order reinforce one another and help create a strong tendency toward compartmentalization in all areas of their lives, for example, inside their dwellings. The open architecture typical of American houses and apartments in which the front door opens into the living room is not common. Walk into a traditional German home or apartment and you will usually find yourself in a small, closed corridor, or *Gang*. This corridor provides access to the other rooms of the house or apartment, and the doors to these other rooms will generally be closed. This configuration is considered orderly, and it also helps reduce heating costs. Because resources are limited, Germans tend to be quite frugal. Most traditional German houses have heating systems that allow them to heat each room separately, leaving unused rooms unheated.

Similarly, doors remain closed in most German public and office buildings, where a closed door does not mean a private meeting is taking place, but only that the door is closed as German notions of orderliness and clear boundaries dictate.

This is a noticeable contrast with the open-door policy of many American businesses. The proper behavior in Germany is to knock and then enter when the person inside responds. Germans say they keep their doors closed so they can get their work done. After all, they argue, you go to work to work; if you want to socialize, go to the movies.

Another example of compartmentalization in German society can be seen in the use of time. Clear and orderly divisions of time organize German life, and specific days and time slots carry an implicit meaning. Thus, to be asked over to someone's house for midafternoon on Sunday automatically implies you are being invited for *Kaffee und Kuchen* (coffee and pastry). At such an event you can expect relaxed conversation accompanied by strong coffee and delicious pastries. Kaffee und Kuchen is just one of various German   that have clearly designated times.

Because of strong regional differences, not all these rituals occur uniformly throughout the entire country. Take, for example, the Swabian *Kehrwoche* (sweeping week). In most parts of Germany, Saturdays are generally the time for washing autos and doing the outside cleaning, but the Swabians have taken this general tendency and institutionalized it. Kehrwoche regulations require that all sidewalks and stairways of apartment buildings be regularly cleaned. In addition the Kehrwoche is a round-robin system in which the inhabitants of each apartment are assigned a particular week during which they are responsible for cleaning the steps and sidewalks of their building. This rotating system of responsibility assures that the cleaning is done and that everyone does the same amount of work. The Swabians seem to easily accept this regulation that promotes the good of the community, even though it places limits on individual freedom. As the section on social obligations later in this chapter will explain, Germans often view giving up certain individual rights as a fair trade in creating a better and more ordered society.

Another example of compartmentalization of time and its effect on the common good is illustrated by the long, drawn-out political discussions about the closing times of German stores. Traditionally stores were only allowed to operate until 6:30 P.M. on weekdays and until 2 P.M. on most Saturdays. Only gas stations and stores in railway stations, as a concession to travelers, could open on Sundays. After years of public debate about extending the stores' hours of operation, they may now stay open until 8 P.M. on weekdays, although many choose not to. One important argument against extending the hours was that longer hours would inconvenience store owners and employees, infringing upon their private time, particularly if they had to work on Sundays. Sunday is considered a *Ruhetag* (day of rest), and Sundays are distinctly different from the hustle and bustle of weekdays. Any activity that makes noise or disturbs the peace, such as mowing the lawn, hammering, or playing loud music, is prohibited. Here, again, notice the German willingness to trade individual rights for social order.

Private and Public Spheres

Germans also compartmentalize the private and public spheres of their lives. As they like to say, *Dienst ist Dienst und Schnaps ist Schnaps* (duty is duty and liquor is liquor), which means that duty and pleasure are not meant to be mixed. While Americans are also known for dividing work from leisure to some extent, Germans carry the separation to a greater degree, not only in their behavior but also in the structure of their language.

Unlike English, German has more than one word for the pronoun *you*. When addressing one another, Germans must choose between using the formal *Sie* and the more familiar *du*. Both mean "you," but each carries significant differences in meaning. To use the wrong form can be highly insulting. Generally speaking, Germans think of a person with whom they work as a *Kollege* (colleague) and not as a friend. For this reason they typically address one another with the formal *Sie*, rather than *du*, which is reserved for friends and family. The deep significance of this distinction for Germans is illustrated by the following episode.

At a large German company where I was employed, there was a manager who refused to come to his department's annual Christmas party. Germans have many holidays, and they typically try to enjoy them with a vengeance, so his behavior struck me as odd. When asked why he didn't attend, he explained that he didn't like socializing with his employees when they were drinking. It wasn't that he had anything against alcohol per se, but he was disturbed by its effects on his employees' behavior. The loosening up that many people experience when they drink, he said, often led the employees to become more friendly and familiar with one another, and sometimes they would lapse into the more familiar *du*. This was fine during the party, but afterward he said he had difficulty maintaining the appropriate distance toward his employees that he felt his job required. To get around this, he simply avoided going to the party. I have since discovered that such behavior is not at all uncommon.

This example shows the clear distinction Germans draw between their private and public lives. Germans value their privacy highly and go to great lengths to protect it. That Germans take their privacy seriously can be seen in their boycott one year of the official census because they were afraid of how the information would be used. It is also reflected in the *Datenschutzgesetz*, strict laws passed to protect against personal data being collected and stored on computers for commercial or government use.

Stephen Kalberg attributes this strong distinction between the private and public spheres in Germany to historical developments significantly different from those in the United States.[3] For Germans the public sphere (work, politics, school, and other places where strangers are likely to meet) was traditionally an area of life dominated by impersonal values related to efficiency, aggressive competition, and ambitious, goal-driven behavior.

On the other hand, the private realm and its attendant values were reserved for people one trusted and knew intimately, that is, for family and friends. In the United States these two realms, the public and the private, tended to merge, serving to mutually influence one another. Thus, a lack of reserve, informality, and friendliness became common to both the private and public spheres in the U.S. In Germany, because these two areas were more compartmentalized, distinct behaviors, values, and expectations developed for each. While formality and reserve are expected in the public sphere, the values of the private sphere are warmth, support, compassion, openness, and humor, all considered totally inappropriate for the public sphere. Many Americans who only know Germans at work are very surprised when they are invited into a German home and then discover this very different side of the German personality.

Friends and Acquaintances

Another facet of the clear compartmentalization of German social life is the strong distinction made between *Freunde* (friends) and *Bekannte* (acquaintances). Many of the people Americans label "friends" would not be considered real friends by Germans. A major distinction between friendship in Germany and in the United States is the degree of commitment and obligation one has toward friends. In Germany friends spend more time together and exhibit a higher degree of commitment and obligation toward one another than do Americans. Mentioning a worry or potential problem to a friend in the U.S. may get the rather vague and optimistic response, "Oh don't worry, you'll do fine." Just hinting to a German friend that there might be a problem will elicit a series of concerned and detailed questions as well as sincere offers of help and support. Such questions may seem intrusive from an American point of view, but for the German, this willingness to get involved in a friend's problems helps define the level of commitment to the friendship.

Because of this sense of obligation that accompanies friendship, Germans limit the number of persons they consider Freunde. They believe that it takes much time and effort to maintain a good friendship and that it is impossible to have more than a few real friends. This is also another factor in their seeming aloofness. They probably already have enough friends and aren't interested in extending their social network. For them the American desire to be popular and to keep as many friends as possible is confusing and seems superficial. As will be discussed in the chapter on business relationships, these different views of friendship can cause misunderstandings when Germans and Americans try to work together.

A major factor in the differences between friendships in Germany and the United States relates to differences in social and geographic mobility. Because Americans are far more mobile geographically and meet more new people when they move, they need to make friends quickly. Not doing so means being lonely. This greater geographic mobility in the U.S. partly explains why many Americans tend to seek their friends among those with whom they work or with whom they attend church. Because Germans separate their private and public lives so clearly, they rarely seek out friendships among their coworkers, nor do they often socialize with them.

Germans, being far less mobile than Americans, may live for generations in the same town, if not the same house. While this has changed somewhat since World War II, most Germans, as said before, are still very attached and loyal to the people of their Heimat. This is one important factor in explaining why many friendships in Germany have been maintained since childhood or college.

In addition to geographic mobility, social mobility also plays a role in creating differences in friendship patterns between Germany and the United States. Americans tend to form friendships on the basis of common interests, and because Americans tend to define their identities more in terms of their occupation than do Germans, work-related interests often determine whom Americans socialize with. As a person's job or position changes, so too do that person's interests and, consequently, social circle. In the U.S. friendships tend to form in large, loose networks of people. Phrases such as "my friend from work," "my bowling friends," or "my buddies from the bar" attest to these wide, relaxed networks of friends, as do "networking" and "working a party." Networks in Germany tend to be smaller, more closed, and more hierarchical than in the U.S. Thus, they limit social mobility and are less susceptible to entry from outsiders.

Although common interests clearly play a role in German friendships, more emphasis is placed on the other person's complete character and personality and whether he or she is *sympathisch* (likable). Rather than looking at only a narrow spectrum of common interests, Germans want to get to know the whole person well before they enter into a friendship. They also want to be able to talk with their friends about a wide range of topics, in particular about their problems, irritations, and upsets. And they want to know if the other person is reliable, trustworthy, and discreet. These character traits are important because of the sense of obligation that is implicit in German friendships.

Clarity and Rational Knowledge as Control

It is no coincidence that the Germans call the Enlightenment the *Aufklärung*, literally, the "period of clearing up." With the Germans' strong sense of history, they view the Enlightenment, with its emphasis on *Wissenschaft* (science and scholarship) and *Vernunft* (rational understanding), as a watershed in human development.

It would be difficult to overestimate the German respect

for understanding based on rational analysis and scientific knowledge, both of which are seen as ways of creating Klarheit. This desire for clarity can be seen in their attempt to define their terms precisely when discussing issues as well as in their love of creating comprehensive categories and taxonomies. Because Germans love to converse at length, clear, well-thought-out, rational arguments based on broad knowledge elicit admiration and great respect. In fact, as we will see in the next chapter, in-depth discussions on just about any subject, politics in particular, are almost as popular as soccer, the national sport.

Displaying one's knowledge while talking is also associated with being educated and thus brings with it not only respect but also status. This is one reason Germans like to appear knowledgeable; it is a way for them to gain credibility and social status. While Germany is now a semiclassless society like the United States, a person's educational background is one of the most direct indicators of that person's status in German society. It is no coincidence that so many company directors and leading politicians hold Ph.D.'s.

Germans also desire clear, unambiguous knowledge as a way to reduce the general insecurity and anxiety that plague them, since having knowledge is one of the best forms of control. From the German perspective, you can only control that which you understand, keeping ever-lurking chaos at bay.

This desire for control through clarity of thought and expression is one of the major factors behind the German tendency for detailed planning. It is not uncommon for Germans in their late teens or twenties to already have life insurance policies as well as plans for their career, financial security, and retirement. They can tell you where they hope to be at each stage of life and what steps they will take to assure their continued well-being and security. Similarly, decision making in German business is marked by clearly laying out all possible contingencies in the beginning stages of a project and then planning all steps of the project accordingly. Improvising, "playing it by ear," and "going with the flow" are too uncertain and ambiguous for the traditional German mindset.

Pflichtbewußtsein

As was seen in the section on friendship, *Pflichtbewußtsein*, or one's sense of duty and obligation, is a major component of the German psyche. In fact the notion of duty and obligation informs the Germans' insider/outsider distinction as well as their strong sense of *Gruppenzugehörigkeit* (group belonging) and *Gemeinschaft* (community). All cultures must deal with the tension between individual rights and personal identity on the one hand, and a person's social role, group identity, and obligations to the larger social group on the other. The United States has radically extended the rights and liberties of the individual more than any other culture in the world. This ethos informs Patrick Henry's famous cry of "Give me liberty or give me death!" While Germans are also strong individualists as well as great believers in the importance of individual rights, they tend to identify more strongly with the groups to which they belong than do Americans. This strong sense of belonging and loyalty to the group goes hand in hand with the sense of duty and obligation they feel toward the common good. It is this idea of being part of a social contract that explains much of the German way of life. Not to fulfill their duty weighs Germans down with a sense of guilt and shame.

The symphony orchestra provides a useful metaphor for Americans wanting to understand this aspect of German culture.[4] While all members of an orchestra must be excellent musicians and highly skilled on a particular instrument, learning to coordinate their playing according to the director's cues and the synchrony of the music is crucial in fulfilling their roles and reaching their common goal—playing a piece of difficult music in an aesthetically pleasing and harmonious way. Egotistical grandstanding or poor playing by an individual musician can ruin the entire performance. For the symphony orchestra to perform well, each individual must willingly submit to the whole in order that a greater good be reached. Unlike jazz, a prototypically American music form characterized by open-ended beginnings and endings and by long, improvised solos by individuals or small groups of musicians "doing their thing," the symphony requires precise planning and complete coordination of many musicians to reach its goal. It is this sense of resolute submission of the individual to the greater good of the collective that typifies much of the German experience and worldview. Americans, of course, have their symphony orchestras, too, but the ideal of the coordinated whole is much rarer in American society. While Germans are clearly not as collectively oriented as many Asian cultures, they have a much stronger sense of social roles and group identity than do Americans.

This sense of submitting to the greater good serves as the main justification for many of the rules and regulations that structure German society. Thus, to break a rule is not only an infraction of the law, it is also a threat to the very notion of the greater good. For this reason many German pedestrians will not cross an intersection against a red light even when no cars are approaching. If asked, they will tell you that respecting the traffic light is a way of showing respect for society and social responsibility in daily life. Furthermore, they will say, to cross against the light would set a bad example for others, particularly children, who might follow their lead and be hit by a car at another crossing.

Perhaps the German sense of obligation finds its roots in the ancient Germanic tribes, whose very survival depended on members working well together. Group solidarity was highly valued, and individuals were severely punished for cowardice or deserting the tribe in times of war. From these earliest times a code of honor and duty developed that shaped Germans' behavior. To really understand this development, one must remember that ever-recurring periods of warfare marked European history, and Germany's central geographic position made it especially vulnerable to the political and military maneuvering of the various European powers. The social evolution of European nations from the tribal stage through feudalism and finally to the class structures which form the basis of current European societies can be understood in part relative to the role of warfare in Europe.

In his outstanding series of historical studies about Germany, *Studien über die Deutschen*, Norbert Elias shows how warfare led to the domination of German society by an aristocracy, which was in effect a warrior class. This warrior class officially controlled Germany until 1918, and their ideals of loyalty, obligation, and courage were adopted by the other classes of German society. Today this sense of obligation and loyalty to the group can be seen in the behavior and sense of affiliation Germans have toward their family, friends, company, and region. It has played a major role in Germany's economic success and is a basic component of the German social market economy, as chapter 5 will illustrate.

The notion of *Verbindlichkeit*, which implies the binding nature of one's word, illustrates another crucial aspect of the German sense of duty and obligation. While still very young, Germans learn to be extremely careful about what they say because they are taught that when they speak, they are committing themselves to what they say. In its most extreme form, Verbindlichkeit is the belief that a person's word reflects upon his or her honor. To not follow through with what one says is to not fulfill one's obligation, something that rightfully causes disrespect in others and feelings of shame in oneself. In a business context, it can make one liable because oral contracts are still legally binding.

The importance of this belief in Verbindlichkeit explains part of the differences in German and American communication styles. Americans are more concerned with pleasing others and so talk accordingly. Germans are more concerned with being both respected and credible. These differences will become clearer in the next chapter, which focuses on German communication style.

---

[1] For more information on German manners and customs, see Susan Stern, *These Strange German Ways*, listed in the References.

[2] "Vorwärts in der Vergangenheit," 73.

[3] Stephen Kalberg, "West German and American Interaction Forms: One Level of Structured Misunderstanding," *Theory, Culture & Society* 4 (1987): 603–18.

[4] In the more religious Middle Ages, Germans, and many Europeans, compared their society to the body of Christ. In this metaphor, each section of society had its function to fulfill if the entire body was to function in good health. Later, in more secular times, this metaphor passed out of usage to be replaced by views of society as an organism or a giant clockwork. What underlies all these metaphors is the notion of a larger whole which can only function well when the individual parts fulfill their roles, thus contributing to the greater good of the whole.

German Communication Patterns[1]

The way we communicate is directly related to the values and norms of the culture in which we are raised, and different cultures tend to prefer different communication styles. Because Germans and Americans use distinctive conversational styles, subtle but significant misunderstandings sometimes occur. Rather than realizing that misperceptions are being caused by communication styles with differing rules and norms, people tend to infer that the other person's inherent character is the cause of the problem. This often results in Americans stereotyping Germans as opinionated and argumentative know-it-alls, while Germans tend to view Americans as naive, superficial, childish, and ignorant. One of the best preparations an American can make for dealing with Germans is to learn about their communication style.

Communication Style

The way people talk and present themselves is in large measure the basis on which we make judgments about their character. We generally assume, based on our perception of a person's demeanor and manner of speaking, that he or she feels or thinks the way we would if we presented ourselves thus. This is not necessarily true. Because we learned to talk and present ourselves as children, much of that behavior is now out of conscious awareness and seems "natural" to us. While we often prepare *what* we are going to say, we rarely think about *how* we will say something unless the situation is clearly critical, such as giving a presentation or going for a job interview. But, in fact, the how is just as important as the what and sends an important message, not only from person to person but also from culture to culture.

Communication style refers to the patterns that we use when we speak. It includes how we organize our presentation, what information we emphasize, how fast we talk, the intonation patterns we use, when we pause, when we interrupt, how and when we smile or gesture, when we use humor or when we apologize, what we assume are the goals of any given interaction, and much more.

For successful intercultural communication to occur, it is useful to understand how we use meaning and language to create our social worlds. It is no coincidence that the words *communicate, community*, and *communion* sound so much alike. They come from the same root and refer to processes of coming together and exchanging and sharing in order to create commonality. Diverse cultures and peoples have had dissimilar histories and resources from which to create their social worlds. In these social worlds, different communication styles are used to coordinate the activities and people of that culture. Understanding this basic fact and being on the lookout for the variations in communication style can improve interactions with Germans immensely.

In Germany there is a strong emphasis on explicit verbal communication, which emphasizes the content level of communication and deemphasizes the relationship level. This is especially so among educated Germans in business and public situations and is directly correlated with the private/public distinction we examined in the previous chapter. Americans also place significant emphasis on the content level of a communication but do not deemphasize the relationship level as much as the Germans do. This different emphasis placed on the content and relationship levels is a major determinant in the distinctions between German and American communication styles.

Educated Germans today have, as we learned in chapter 3, idealized rational, analytical knowledge, and their communication style tends to be explicit, fact-oriented, and academic. There is a widespread belief among well-educated Germans that only by remaining rational and by consistently following clear principles will humans be able to achieve a better, more civilized society. Germans also believe that to really express something exactly, one needs complicated language. This leads to a business German that is more elevated and convoluted as compared with the more pragmatic, popularistic American style.

Corresponding to the strong emphasis on content, the relationship aspects of communication, as mentioned before, are more marginalized. Conflict is generally avoided, not by emphasizing harmony in personal relationships or by smoothing over differences of opinion, but rather by maintaining formality and social distance. *Direct attacks on the content of a person's communication are common, but attacks on the person are avoided by keeping the discussion impersonal and objective.*

While the ideal is to strive for rational objectivity, this does not mean that Germans avoid topics that raise the temperature and tensions in the group. Heated discussions are, in fact, quite common, and many become overly combative from an American's viewpoint. From a German perspective, however, such discussions are still quite within the bounds of normal communication.

This point was driven home to me while sitting in a beer garden with three German friends. We were enjoying the late afternoon of a pleasant spring day and killing some time before leaving for a party. As so often happens in groups of Germans, the relaxed conversation became serious as talk turned to politics. State elections were coming up and Elke, Rudi, and Thorsten were discussing the candidates and issues. When Thorsten made it clear he had no intention of voting, the level of the conversation changed. Rather than dropping the subject, as would most likely have occurred in the United States, Rudi and Elke went on the offensive, actively trying to persuade Thorsten that it was his duty to vote and brandishing a wide range of arguments to support their position. Thorsten for his part remained adamant that his vote would not change anything.

This example of a prototypical German discussion went on for about twenty minutes. The intensity and vigor with which both sides made their arguments and the directness with which they expressed themselves were uncomfortable to my American sensibilities. Their voices rose, their body movements became more energetic, and they continually interrupted one another. The atmosphere seemed suddenly quite charged. If they had been Americans, I would have been uneasy and worried that they would go away angry or perhaps even become violent. However, having witnessed such talks between German friends before, I was not especially concerned. And I was not at all surprised when Elke broke off the talk to remind us it was almost seven o'clock and that we should move on if we didn't want to be late for the party. The subject was dropped, and we left for the party with no sign of animosity or vindictive reserve on the part of any of the three friends. In fact we spent the rest of the evening and early morning hours together, thoroughly enjoying ourselves. The fact that this discussion took place among close friends is of major import in the way the conversation was enacted. The intensity, directness, and informality used by the three correlates strongly with their close friendship and their age (early thirties) and with their use of the informal mode of address, that is, the *du* mode. Had they been older, in a more formal setting, or not known one another so well, they would have probably used the more formal mode of address, the *Sie* mode.

Du and Sie Revisited

The use of the formal *Sie* (use of last names and titles, verbs in the third person, and a more distanced, less emotional style of speaking) differs significantly from the informal *du* and strongly influences the way people converse in Germany. As was shown in the last chapter, this distinction is an accurate mirror of German culture as well as a major parameter of the German communication style.

Kurt Lewin[2] was one of the first social scientists to conceive of the individual personality as being interwoven with, and partially structured by, the sociocultural system in which that person was raised. He considered certain personality types or structures as being correlated with particular sociocultural systems. Expanding on his idea of using concentric circles to visually represent prototypical personalities in the United States and Germany, we can better see how the *du/Sie* distinction is a major factor in German and American communication   styles.

Figure 1: General Model of Self

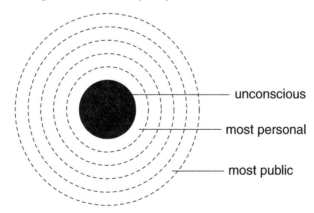

In Figure 1, the inner circles represent the most personal, intimate, and vulnerable parts of a person. These private parts are only divulged to one's family and closest friends—or to doctors, therapists, and priests—if at all. The outward concentric circles represent the more public, less personal parts of a person. These outer circles, or layers, contain those subjects and behaviors a person is least shy about and most willing to divulge in public. In Germany and the United States significant differences exist between these layers of privacy and openness. These differences are not biological but are learned in childhood, as a child grows up and interacts with family, friends, and society.

Figure 2: U.S. Selves Interacting

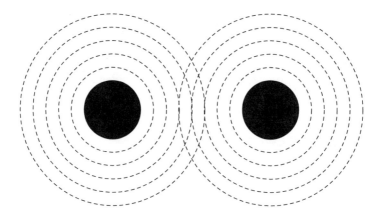

The typical U.S. personality structure (Figure 2) is marked by layers of increasing intimacy which have only vaguely delineated boundaries. This represents the extroversion of Americans and their willingness to quickly move to a first-name basis, as well as a tendency to talk quite openly about many things that people from Germany regard as highly personal. Despite this friendliness, however, the majority of U.S. interactions are limited by a large center of information that is considered private and out-of-bounds for normal interactions.

Figure 3: **German Sie Interaction**

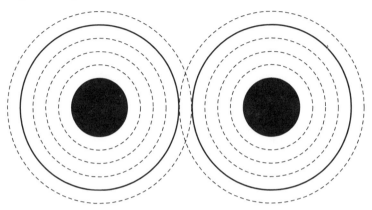

In the German model (as represented in Figure 3), there is a clear, strong boundary very near the surface, which is represented in this diagram by the thick dark line and which corresponds to the private/public distinction. In other words, this boundary very clearly distinguishes the parts of a German considered public and private, and it corresponds quite directly with the *du/Sie* distinction. Most German interactions between people will not penetrate past the outer layers of the personality (Sie).

In the U.S. model there is no such sharp distinguishing line, just as in English there is only one personal pronoun, *you*, and thus much more overlap or openness and friendliness in the majority of interactions. Whereas in Germany the strong outer boundary, the *du/Sie* line, keeps most interactions fairly reserved and formal (Sie), for those persons that one has a closer relationship with (du), the areas of the personality that interact are in fact larger than in the United States, as is shown in Figure 4. This is because the areas that Germans consider totally off-limits to friends and family is smaller. Because Germans make such clear distinctions between *du* and *Sie* relationships and because Americans do not, misunderstandings are bound to occur in many German and American relationships, both at work and socially.

Figure 4: **German Du Interaction**

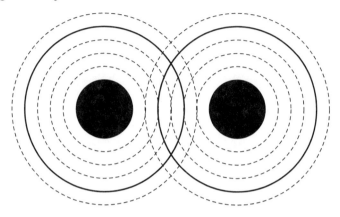

In my research into German communication patterns, I conducted many interviews with Germans. Once, while trying to clearly understand the rules for using *du* and *Sie*, my own desire for simplicity and ease conflicted with the complexity of the German system. In frustration I asked my informant why the Germans couldn't make it simple and just use one second-person pronoun as English speakers do. Ignoring the obvious ethnocentrism, my German friend answered with typical German irony, "*Warum einfach, wenn es auch kompliziert geht?*" (Why simple, when we can make it complicated?). People who say the Germans don't have a sense of humor simply don't understand them.

Understanding the social conventions that underlie the use of *du* and *Sie* is not simple, especially because they are not static, having changed significantly in the last fifty years. Until the 1960s, adult Germans who did not know one another well were expected to use the *Sie* form of personal address and a person's last name. Not to do so constituted an insulting sign of disrespect. It is therefore typical for most relationships between adult Germans to at least begin with *Sie*. Among adults, the criterion for deciding whether to use *du* or *Sie* has traditionally been the degree of familiarity between the persons speaking. Put simply, if they knew one another well and had achieved a certain degree of trust, they might switch to *du* and first names. To switch to the *du* form requires mutual consent and is accomplished explicitly by saying something like "*Wollen wir uns nicht duzen?*" (Shouldn't we say *du* to one another?) or, for older, more traditional Germans, "*Wollen wir Brüderschaft trinken?*" (Shall we drink to brotherhood?). This mutuality is important.[3] If one of the speakers is not in agreement, using the more familiar *du* form creates big problems. In many cases, especially in the workplace, adults never switch to the *du* form, preferring to maintain the respect, formality, and distance that go with *Sie*. Staying on a *Sie* level is also a way of telling neighbors to maintain the proper distance. And staying on a *Sie* level is also a way to avoid the ambiguity and risk that can occur in negotiating a closer relationship.

Traditional German adults expect children to say *Sie* to them, while they in turn address children with *du*. This asymmetric usage reflects perceptions of differences in status. When calling animals, as might be expected, Germans also use the *du* form.

In the lower grades at school, teachers are addressed with *Sie*, while they address their students with *du*. When German students turn sixteen, the law requires their teachers to address them with *Sie*. This is a rite of passage for the students and a big moment in their lives.

However, cultures and languages are in a continual state of flux, and the German culture—as with most cultures of the Western world—went through some turbulent transitions in the 1960s. As mentioned in chapter 2, the student movement and the Generation of '68 set about to change Germany, and in some ways they succeeded.

Until the 1960s, it was typical for all university students who didn't know one another well to address each other with *Sie*. Then members of the student movement began intentionally addressing one another with *du* as a sign of group solidarity. By doing so they were imitating the unions and socialists who had already been using the *du* form to create a sense of solidarity among their members. Since that period, it has become common for younger Germans to address one another with *du* whenever they meet in a nonprofessional situation. This looser use of *du* by younger Germans is just one manifestation of the large generation gap that exists in Germany.

Today, Germans must take two major criteria into account when deciding whether to use *du* or *Sie*: how well they know someone and whether they perceive the other person as a member of their group or not. What had once been simple and straightforward has now become so complicated that even some Germans admit they sometimes don't know which form to use.

Private/Public Revisited

As should now be clear, the *du/Sie* distinction correlates positively with the private/public distinction and greatly influences most aspects of German communication style. Thus it is more common to hear *Sie* in the office, unless the company is small and all the employees know one another, or if the office is staffed by young employees. But in leisure activities, such as the innumerable German sports clubs, *du* is heard more frequently. In fact, it is not uncommon for some Germans to say *Sie* to one another in the office and then use *du* when together in private. To be able to read between the lines of German communication, Americans must understand that the use of *du* or *Sie* is not simply a change of verbs and pronouns but rather a major change in modality. It is as noticeable as the distinction between the major and minor scales played on a piano. By making minimal grammatical changes, speakers introduce a whole different mood and modality.

Because English no longer has such a clear distinction, the widespread use of first names and the generally friendly manner of Americans, especially those in the service industries, initially cause confusion among Germans. This is an example of linguistic interference which causes them to confuse the general openness and friendly style of Americans with the openness and warmth they associate with *du* relationships at home. And when they discover that most Americans are just being friendly in the way typical of their communication style and do not want a deeper friendship, Germans tend to stereotype Americans as "superficial."

On the other hand, if they are aware that use of first names and a friendly approach are simply part of a widespread American social style, they then tend to remain in their *Sie* mode. This comes across to Americans as cold, distant, and at times arrogant, leading them to perceive Germans in terms of negative stereotypes.

In my seminars designed to promote better understanding between Germans and Americans, I often do a stereotype exercise with the Americans. I ask them what comes to mind when they think of Germans. Without fail, three images of Germans emerge time after time: as boisterous beer drinkers, dressed in lederhosen and enthusiastically enjoying the Oktoberfest; as producers of excellent automobiles and other high-quality industrial products; or as Nazis. When asked where these stereotypes come from, most agree these images are common in the media as well as in stories and anecdotes they had heard growing up.

Because these images and stereotypes are floating around in the back of our minds, it is all too easy to misinterpret the German style of speech, thinking it is the character of the person talking and not merely the style of communication the culture expects. In truth, while most Americans prefer a friendly smile to a frown, many put on a smile even when they are not feeling especially friendly, in part because their communication style emphasizes the relationship side of communication, encouraging them to be outgoing and person-able. Another reason is the strong emphasis placed on cus-tomer service in the United States; that is, you get more sales with honey than with vinegar. And because Americans don't distinguish as strictly between insiders and outsiders as do Germans, they tend to use this friendly style more frequently and with more people. Everyone knows, though, that smiling faces sometimes hide more than they reveal and that the friendliness of a telemarketer is purely bogus.

Developing trust is a key component of successful commu-nication, and we intuitively tend to trust those who use the same style of communication as we do. This is partially be-cause we understand the assumptions from which they are operating, and thus their communication seems more natu-ral, more logical to us. With such people we don't have to make as much effort to read between the lines but can deal more directly with the issues at hand.

Directness and Klarheit

Directness is a powerful communicative signal. It varies ac-cording to power and status and from culture to culture. Ameri-cans tend to think of themselves as very direct and to the point. Compared with many cultures, they are. Compared with Germans they are less so, although this depends on the situa-tion and the particular speech act. In giving compliments or expressing pleasure or positive emotions, Americans are often more direct, especially in public. And as regards disclosing personal details to people they don't know well, Americans can also be much more direct than Germans. But in terms of stating facts, offering criticism, and issuing direct commands, Germans are generally more direct, leading to perceptions of them as opinionated, blunt, and brusque know-it-alls.

As mentioned earlier, directness and honesty are highly valued by Germans and thus among the most telling charac-teristics of their style of speech. Part of this emphasis on directness is related to their desire for *Klarheit* and dislike of ambiguity.

The commonly heard idiom, *Jetzt werde ich mit ihm Deutsch reden müssen* (Now I'll have to speak German with him), shows just how central this idea is to German speakers. When this idiom is used, it doesn't imply the partners were previously speaking to each other in a foreign language, but rather that an unacceptable situation has developed and it's time to stop beating around the bush. Or as another common phrase has it, "It's time to speak *Klartext*" (clearly or directly). Perhaps it is only coincidence, but the German adjective *deutlich* (clear, plain, distinct) as well as the German verb *deuten* (explain, expound, interpret) is morphologically very similar to the word Germans use to refer to themselves and their language: *Deutsch*.

The desire for clarity in German speech leads to directness that is sometimes off-putting to foreigners. A brief examination of some of their microlevel verbal habits will help clarify this aspect of German speaking style. Linguists use the term *downgraders* to denote words that make an expression weaker and less definite, while *upgraders* do just the reverse. Examples of some American downgraders are *sort of, kind of, pretty much, maybe, well,* and so on. While Germans typically use upgraders when complaining, many Americans soften criticism by using downgraders. Thus, in criticizing the campaign financing scandal of the Clinton administration, one of my American friends downgraded his statement, making it less direct by saying, "Well, it doesn't show him in a real positive light." A German friend, on the other hand, was more direct, concluding, *"Das war absolut unverschämt"* (That was absolutely shameless). Calling someone "shameless" is quite common and comes from the more absolutist moral values typical of traditional German culture. This more absolute approach is expressed by the use of upgraders, words and phrases such as *definitely, absolutely, totally, without a doubt,* and so on, which strengthen an expression.

A second common German verbal habit, the use of un-qualified yes or no statements, often leads to misperceptions on the part of Americans, who are more accustomed to giving less direct answers. Ask a German a question to which he or she has a yes or no answer, and you will get a direct yes or no response. To them it seems simple enough. You asked a direct question and he or she is giving you a direct, clear answer, with no harm intended. Often the answer will also include a detailed explanation or argument to defend the answer. Germans are cautious, however, and are usually unwilling to answer a question without giving it appropriate thought.

Direct contradictions are a third verbal tool Germans don't shy away from. If you make a statement and a German con-tradicts you without blinking, don't be surprised. In fact, the primary function of *doch*, one of the most frequently used words in German, is to contradict the previous thought. While *ja* means "yes," so does doch, but only as a form of contradiction. German children learn to use this word very early in their verbal development. For example, were a parent to tell his or her child that candy really isn't healthful, it is quite likely the child would reply with a firm "Doch!" (Yes it is!). Germans practice stating their opinions clearly from an early age.

Fourth, Germans tend to use the modal verbs *müssen* (must) and *sollen* (should) somewhat differently and more frequently than Americans do, which can also make their style seem stronger and less diplomatic. Thus, a German would not think it odd to say *"Das muß so sein"* (It must be that way), where an American might express this opinion more diplo-matically as "It would be good if we could do it that way." Similarly, Germans tend to use direct imperatives more fre-quently than do Americans; for example, in a restaurant a customer might simply say *"Bringen Sie uns zwei Rotwein, bitte"* (Bring us two red wines, please), whereas an American might use a question format instead: "Could we have two glasses of red wine please?"

Taken together, these verbal habits can create the impression that Germans are overly confrontational speakers who are not very concerned with the image they are creating. This is a false perception. All communication has a component of self-representation or image management, and German is no exception. Germans are very concerned about the image they present during a conversation, but the positive images they aspire to are somewhat different from those Americans try to create. In general, because of the strong public/private distinction, Germans strive for credibility and respect when speaking in the public sphere. At home and with friends, credibility is still important, but then likableness and affection play a much greater role in influencing speech style.

Critical Questions

Intellectual criticism plays a central role in German speech patterns and has a long and honorable history. Starting with Kant's *Critique of Pure Reason* and continuing through Marx and Engels' examination of European society, criticism has served as one of the main forces in liberating Europeans from superstition and despotism. Asking critical and incisive questions based on a certain skepticism served as a call to action during the Enlightenment. From this perspective, being critical is also a way to be socially responsible. Of course during the Hitler period, a critical bent was not popular with the Nazis.

After World War II this critical force reemerged and served as a major component in revitalizing and democratizing German society. At that time, many intellectuals, political activists, and students felt it socially responsible to ask questions critical of their culture and government. The thoroughness and integrity with which they were willing to examine and question their past was unique in history.[4] This critical review of their past was the subject of novels, plays, public debate, and television and radio programs. The student movement and its focus on the Nazi past were discussed in count-less news broadcasts and thus became the frequent subject of dining table discussions. Many older Germans were extremely disturbed by the intensity with which the younger generation pursued the issue. Families were divided by heated arguments, and a lasting generation gap ensued, as discussed earlier.

One of the conclusions arrived at by the intellectuals and students was that Hitler and the Nazis could only have come to power because of ignorance and a lack of social commitment on the part of ordinary Germans. The denial of this proposition by many older Germans only strengthened the younger generation's belief in the need for a critical assessment of the Nazi era. While the fervor of this debate has died down, it has left its mark. Today many Germans, particularly those on the left and in the younger generation, still speak quite openly and critically about their nation's past. They have deep issues with regard to their national identity, and they find the patriotism and nationalistic tendencies of many Americans naive and troublesome. For them criticism is part of political liberation and the creation of a better society. Since they find it normal to criticize their own culture, they don't understand Americans' defensive reactions to criticism about American policy and culture. Germans often complain that they can't have a satisfying political discussion with Americans because they become defensive when Germans follow their critical bent. From the American perspective, Germans are not only overly critical of American politics, they are also perceived as being pessimistic and unwilling to become enthusiastic in the typical American style.

This centuries-long history of applying critical intelligence to public issues has become an integral part of German communication style and thus has a very different meaning for them than it does for Americans. This was demonstrated to me at a conference. An American speaker had just finished his presentation and was fielding questions. A series of penetrating questions came from several of the Germans present. The questioning dealt with some ethical issues and increased in intensity as the American became less sure of himself. My sympathy went out to the speaker, who began to look more and more like bait for some very hungry sharks. A German friend offered a different perspective when I mentioned the incident to him. He thought the presentation had generally been good but that there were some important gaps that had necessarily been exposed. When I referred to the loss of face for the presenter, he said people were socially obligated to get to the truth, but not necessarily to save face. And besides, if the Germans had felt the presentation was not generally worthwhile, they certainly wouldn't have wasted their time asking such critical questions. From his perspective those questions signaled interest, not rejection.

Diskussion

Critical questions play a major part in one of the most common genres of German conversation, the *Diskussion* (discussion). Germans love to discuss just about anything under the sun. Diskussion is by its very nature goal-oriented and therefore to be taken seriously, and while Diskussion can be found in both the public and private spheres, it occurs much more frequently in the public sphere. The goals of Diskussion can be to test one's knowledge, discover the truth, or solve some problem, and, one hopes, to come to some consensus with one's conversation partner in the process. Mostly, Diskussion is analytical in nature and focuses on an issue that Germans consider a problem. From their perspective, the way to solve a problem is to completely understand it, which also means understanding its causes and other relevant background details. This mindset leads Germans to prefer a historical approach that looks at the interrelationships of all the different aspects of the issue. It is not uncommon in a Diskussion to track an issue back for centuries, which is another example of

German thoroughness and strong appreciation for the past. Americans, with their more pragmatic and future-oriented mindset, often take a "Don't tell me the problem, tell me the solution" approach, which Germans find intellectually unsatisfactory. This discomfort with each other's approach to problem solving plays an important role in business, as the section on decision making in chapter 6 illustrates.

Another aspect of Diskussion is the level of objectivity and seriousness expected. In a Diskussion one is expected to be as impersonal, serious, and objective as possible. This, of course, precludes any banter or attempts at humor, which are considered inappropriate. In the German education system similar behavior and attitudes are expected in class, resulting in a more intellectual atmosphere. A German friend, while training as a graduate teaching assistant at a major American university, told me how shocked he was upon being instructed to intentionally use jokes in order to loosen up the classroom atmosphere. Such behavior went against all he had learned as appropriate classroom protocol.

Unterhaltung and Gemütlichkeit

Unterhaltung has no satisfactory direct translation into English. One of the closest is simply "conversation," but Unterhaltung is also synonymous with "entertainment," and in the German mind they are often one and the same. Sitting around after a good meal or over a cup of coffee and talking for hours is pure pleasure for Germans. For them it is a way to test their knowledge and become more informed, while at the same time getting to know one another better and cementing bonds of friendship. They simply don't understand how Americans can come to dinner and then not remain for hours afterward to talk unless they hadn't enjoyed the group's company. And perhaps worse, being invited to an American's home and then sitting in the living room while a TV or a video provides the entertainment seems to a German the sign of a poor education or outright ignorance as well as disrespect for the guest. For Germans the conversation itself is sufficient entertainment. Unterhaltung is distinguished by its relative lightness and lack of intensity. It typically has no goal other than the enjoyment of the very act of conversation. Humor is welcomed in an Unterhaltung; in fact an Unterhaltung among friends in a private house is usually filled with laughter, warmth, and a jovial atmosphere, which gives rise to a highly enjoyable state that Germans describe as *gemütlich*, roughly translated as "cozy, congenial, jolly, hearty."

Such situations often surprise foreigners. They discover a much warmer, laughing side to German colleagues who seemed so serious and grim at the office. Evenings spent with Germans in their homes are often filled with laughter, playful teasing, and a warm comradery and trust that are rare in the United States. But if an important topic comes up, the mood can also change and rapidly become serious. The mood will only become jovial again when the topic has been thoroughly dealt with. To switch back to the lightness too quickly might be interpreted as a lack of commitment.

Vertiefen: *Going into Detail*

To achieve their analytical ends Germans use a strategy called *vertiefen*, or "going into depth." The procedure is to try to discover the core or central aspect of a question, issue, or problem, and to do this they employ theoretical arguments, statements of fact, and critical questions. In these discussions one sees the thoroughness and exactness for which they are well known. Needless to say, considerations of saving face are secondary to the goal at hand—discovering the truth.

This leads to an explicit style of speech in which precision of expression, exactness of definition, and literalness play important parts. These different expectations regarding details and precision lead to further reinforcement of already-existing stereotypes. Americans perceive Germans as perfectionistic and compulsive; they see Americans as superficial and slipshod.

Contributing to these stereotypes is the higher degree of free association common in American conversations. Perhaps because Americans value creativity and imagination so highly, they tend to jump more from topic to topic when conversing. This is in direct contradiction to the German strategy of vertiefen, which requires that the speakers stay on topic until some resolution is achieved.

This strategy leads to long, detailed discussions that sometimes go on for hours. Germans want great amounts of detailed information, whether it's for making a business decision, drawing up plans for the next vacation, or simply buying consumer goods. How prevalent this attitude is can be seen in German advertising, which is filled with details, facts, and technical specifications. This relates to their idea of thoroughness; that is, if you're going to do something, do it well or don't do it at all. They want to know small details that Americans often find superfluous and boring. In general, Germans also want lots of details because they distrust simplicity. They tend to suspect that if a thing is not complicated, then something important is missing.

Some Americans find such discussions enjoyable, but many find them tedious and drawn-out and at times threatening. Germans also enjoy such talks, in which they shy away less from delicate issues like religion, politics, and sex than do Americans. This is something Germans miss when trying to have a satisfactory conversation with Americans, who are less willing to express different points of view, or at least to express them so bluntly.

Germans[5] do not necessarily like controversy more than Americans, but they shy away from it less. They share a widespread belief that it is important to be informed and to have an opinion, especially as regards politics. Not to do so is seen as a sign of poor character—and this is not only so among the highly educated Germans. Even among working-class people, talking about politics and other controversial issues is a common pastime. From the German perspective, having a good—even if somewhat confrontational—discussion allows the conversationalists to get to know one another better as well as helping them understand the world a little more. People who rarely express a clear point of view are viewed negatively as *glatt* (slippery), or "lacking format."

While many Americans tend to find argumentation among friends invasive and upsetting, Germans see it as part of the obligation one friend has to another. This involvement can extend into personal realms as well. For example, if a German is dating someone whom a friend feels is not a worthy person, that friend may tell him or her so. Such advice on personal affairs can lead to arguments, but most Germans accept that as part of the price they pay for having good, reliable friends. The bottom line seems to be that Americans strive harder for harmony in interpersonal relationships, while Germans tend to place more emphasis on directness and honesty. Germans also like harmony but are less averse to minor confrontations and seem more practiced in dealing with them.

Verbindlichkeit

Part of the reason Germans are so exact relates to their notion of what is *verbindlich* (binding, obligatory, or compulsory). We have noted before that as children, Germans are taught that they should think carefully before speaking because their word represents their honor. Or to put it another way, they are committed to do that which they say they will do. This underlying sense that they will be held accountable for what they say permeates German speech. It also relates strongly to their desire to be seen as credible and worthy of respect. To say something and then not carry through with it is a blemish on one's reputation.

Perhaps, as some older Germans complain, younger Germans are less verbindlich than previous generations; nevertheless, Verbindlichkeit is still an important force in structuring German speech style. This is important for Americans to know because of their philosophy of "keeping one's options open," "maintaining a flexible position," and "going with the flow," which leads to a more tolerant approach when people change their minds or decisions. Balancing commitment and flexibility can be a dilemma for Americans. As a German friend of mine once said, "I think you Americans talk about commitment so much because you don't have very much of it. In Germany we don't talk about it much because it's simply expected."

When dealing with Germans, it is important for Americans to remember that their standards and expectations regarding commitment differ from those of their German colleagues. For one thing, oral contracts are still legally binding in Germany. Many business deals have gone sour because of misperceptions regarding unkept delivery dates and other matters that the German thought were agreed upon and that the American thought had been talked about only as a possibility. And in the private sphere, Germans are far less forgiving of people who change plans at the last minute or won't commit to doing something. Credibility and reliability are key points that Germans are looking for in both personal and business relationships.

Similarly, open-ended phrases, which in the United States are intended to lubricate a social interaction but are not seriously meant, such as "I'll give you a call" or "Let's have lunch sometime," are also confusing and disturbing for Germans, who tend to interpret such phrases literally.

Referring to commitment in a training seminar, one German manager said, "First I say no, then I consider whether I might be able to say yes. But I always hesitate before agreeing to do something or committing myself. Otherwise I could get myself in a jam." Others agreed that they, too, used this strategy. Verbindlichkeit brings with it an attitude of caution and thus helps keep discussions from becoming overly confrontational, as does the German notion of *Sachlichkeit*.

Sachlichkeit

Translated literally, *Sachlichkeit* means "objectivity," but for Germans it means far more. It is really a mode or style of speaking and means sticking to the matter at hand, leaving out any personal references, and being as unemotional and matter-of-fact as possible. The idea of being *sachlich* pervades German speech, especially in the public sphere.

Sachlichkeit is reflected in the frequent use of *man* (one) and impersonal formulations beginning with *es* (it) as in, *Es versteht sich, daß man so etwas nicht tut* (It is obvious that one shouldn't do that). These and similar formulations abound in standard German, and this propensity to use what might be called "it" language is encouraged in the schools and expected in educated speech. Such "it" language gives educated German talk a sense of being highly impersonal, abstract, and objective, all of which make confrontations more formal and less likely to become overly heated. Such formal, impersonal style is more common among middle and upper classes, who tend to speak standard German.

Along with such impersonal formulations, Germans are taught to think of their opinions as something distinct from their person. By dissociating opinion from person, Germans attempt to be more objective and also tend to be more intellectual and content-oriented. German schools reinforce Sachlichkeit as an integral part of their writing program; most German pupils have had practice in defending positions they don't personally agree with. This tends to sharpen their argumentation skills as well as helping them maintain a certain psychological distance from their opinions. Thus they seem more comfortable with having their opinions attacked, without seeing it as an attack on their person. Again, this kind of impersonal abstract talk is interpreted as coldness and aloofness by many Americans.

When communicating with Americans, Germans feel they constantly have to be on the alert not to offend, because Americans tend to react personally when their opinions are attacked. They feel dissatisfied with conversations in which one side is constantly evading direct confrontation in order to maintain a harmonious relationship. In fact, many Germans, especially men, will tell you they find conversations in which everyone agrees boring. They say that the points of disagreement are the most interesting and are where they can learn or teach something. Of course, this applies in an ideal situation. In fact, many times neither person seems to be trying to learn from the other; each is more intent on proving that his or her position is right. Taken together, these different approaches to discussion often leave both Germans and Americans confused and dissatisfied.

Another aspect of remaining sachlich is keeping one's personal stories and experiences out of the conversation as much as possible. Here German notions of modesty and Sachlichkeit reinforce one another to make the talk more objective and as impersonal as possible. The American penchant for personalizing the discussion is looked upon by Germans with both distaste and envy. On the one hand, they find it quite amazing that Americans can talk about themselves so much, so openly, and so naturally and may find themselves wishing they could do the same. On the other hand, they often view this focus on the self as unfounded bragging. One German friend cited the example of an American who answered yes when asked if he spoke Spanish. When it turned out this fellow had only had one year of college Spanish and could barely utter two complete sentences in Spanish, my friend was amazed. From her perspective, a person would only say he or she could do something if, in fact, he or she were quite competent in that area.

Since emotions are generally considered a disturbance to the objectivity of a conversation, Germans attempt to limit the appearance of emotion in most discussions that take place in the public sphere. A major exception to this rule of thumb is the expression of irritation or annoyance.

The Fine Art of Complaining

In 1936 Kurt Lewin noted that Germans more commonly expressed their annoyance and irritation than did Americans, and his claim is still true today and can be a major cause of misunderstanding when Germans and Americans try to communicate. Remembering that when we are communicating, we are using words for a purpose, we might ask "What are Germans doing when they complain?" And it is just as helpful to ask "Why don't Americans do the same?"

From one point of view, expressing criticism and complaint can be viewed as a continuum. They both involve making negative remarks about someone or something, but they are viewed somewhat differently by Germans. Perhaps freedom of speech and the attendant right to criticize the powers that be is something Germans do not take for granted. Or perhaps criticism is just an integral part of the German philosophical tradition. Witness the enormously influential trilogy by Kant: *Critique of Pure Reason*, *Critique of Practical Reason*, and *Critique of Judgment*. Part of this legacy is that criticism is seen as a right that must be well protected and reaffirmed through continual use. Criticism has a long intellectual pedigree in Germany and is often viewed as something both useful and necessary for the smooth functioning of a business or society. Complaining, on the other hand, is often viewed rather negatively by Germans, and yet, the fact is they spend large amounts of their time and energy doing just that. This fact can be illustrated by the number of words in German that exist to describe the act: *klagen, sich beklagen, nörgeln, sich beschweren, mäkeln, schimpfen, wettern, jammern,*

86

meckern, motzen. While each has its nuances, they all relate to the common act of complaining.

This is perhaps not so surprising when we realize that all cultures contain inherent contradictions that don't seem to be interpreted as contradictions by the members of those cultures. Consider American culture. Certainly freedom and individual liberty are values that all Americans would agree are the foundations of society; they are written into the Constitution. And yet, the United States has incarcerated more of its citizens than any other industrialized country in the world. Many Americans do not see that as a contradiction at all, because they don't think of these persons as "citizens" but rather as "criminals." But to the outside world, this seems a pronounced contradiction.

So what are Germans doing socially when they are complaining? To understand their complaining it is useful to understand what anthropologist George Foster called the "image of limited good."[6] Put in the simplest of terms, the image of limited good is based on the notion of a *zero sum game* in which all resources come in a limited supply. Thus, not only is there a limited amount of gold, oil, land, water, and so on in our world, but also love, safety, happiness, and other nontangibles are in limited supply. Taking too much of any of these resources leaves too little for others. This notion and the corresponding idea that each person gets a fair share only when others don't take more than their share is the fundamental assumption underlying much of the complaining one hears among Germans. Having an abundance of resources arouses other people's envy and wrath, and Germans try carefully to avoid triggering such reactions. Given that many resources are in fact limited, it is easy to see why in such a densely populated country as Germany such an ethos would become widespread.

In the United States, an assumption of unlimited good is more common, and complaining is less socially acceptable. Quite probably the American penchant for optimism combined with the open-frontier mentality served to keep complaining to a minimum. Complaining too much in the United States will get you branded very quickly as a loser and a whiner, and so most Americans try to avoid it.

Germans are encouraged to be modest and not flaunt their wealth and success. Understatement, not bragging, is valued. And one exaggerated form of understatement is complaining. Ask a German businessman how his company is doing and you will often hear about the problematic state of the economy, the increase in competition, the new regulations that are making production more complicated, the difficult problems the company is encountering, and so on. But if you look at his company's profit and loss statement, you will often be surprised to see the company is well in the black, with good prospects for the future. Much of this type of complaining is simply the socially required "modesty" and "realism" that are expected in Germany—as well as an attempt to camouflage success so as not to arouse envy on the part of others. This is very different from the American corporate scene, where one is expected to present a positive image and where talking about problems is frowned upon. In fact many Americans state they have no problems, only "challenges" and "issues."

But complaining in Germany is more than just camouflaging success. It is also a social ritual for building a relationship and creating community. In the United States when two strangers meet, they will often engage in small talk. Part of what they are doing is trying to find things they have in common, which can then serve as the basis for further conversation and a deepening of the relationship. This search for commonalities was important in a land of immigrants. There were obviously differences between them, so looking for common ground was crucial to building a relationship.

In Germany the situation was quite different. Rather than a loosely linked, diverse mass of people who were both socially and geographically mobile, German society was ethnically homogeneous, old, and well established, with a clear social structure in which everyone was firmly embedded. There was little need to seek information about who the other person was, because most likely you knew the other person rather well, or at least could guess quite accurately what he or she was like, depending on behavior and attire. In this society, complaining became a social ritual and a way to establish a sense of commonality and social solidarity. Today this old ritual continues unabated. Sit down with some people who rent apartments—because of the high population, land is at a premium in Germany and far more people rent in Germany than in the United States—and one of the themes of conversation will be criticism directed at landlords for trying to raise the rent or for not keeping the place maintained properly. Sit down with the landlords, however, and you will hear a very different story. They will complain about how their costs have soared and how they are losing money because of rent control laws. Furthermore, they will tell you how they would like to get rid of at least some of their tenants but cannot because they are so well protected by the law. The litany seems to continue endlessly, while the American sits there wondering how people who never stop complaining have ever managed to achieve so much, which misses the crucial point that complaining is a social ritual and not a sign of despair.

Through complaining together and about the same topics, the speakers are implicitly communicating that they belong to the same group and thus share a common view and common interests. The art of complaining is still highly valued in Germany, because while it has abolished its official class system and is now only a semiclassless society, class boundaries and rankings still play an important role. Establishing one's social position is an important part of communication, and what one complains about says a lot about one's social position.

Complaining also serves as an emotional safety valve. German society is quite competitive, and this competition combined with a high population density creates a sense of social pressure and claustrophobia, which many Germans don't manage well. Getting together with one's friends to complain is a way to vent this emotional pressure. And because they come to understand one another's problems better, they often feel more favorably disposed toward one another, thus creating stronger bonds of friendship. Mention to a German friend that you have a problem and your friend will take time to ask lots of detailed questions to figure out what the problem is and how to help you.

One of the results of the German strategy of mutual commiseration is that friends tend to divulge far more of their private affairs to one another than Americans do. Americans tend to carefully weigh just what information they are giving away, perhaps because they know that once it has been spoken, there is no way to recall it. And because Americans are involved in more, larger, and looser social networks than Germans, that information could end up causing embarrassment. Because friendships are entered into more slowly and cautiously, Germans have been able to carefully test their friends' discretion and know they can be trusted. If this trust has been abused in the past, then the relationship will probably have been dissolved.

That American friends don't spend as much time complaining or commiserating over their problems strikes Germans as odd for several reasons. First, they interpret this fact as a sign that Americans aren't being completely honest. Germans have trouble believing that Americans are really always so optimistic, so "up" or so "on" all the time, especially when their verbal and nonverbal behaviors don't seem to match. This sends a mixed message, and sometimes distrust stems simply from the Americans' lack of negativity, which the Germans see as unnatural. Secondly, they miss the feelings of trust and solidarity that are generated through commiserating with friends. One German I spoke to even suggested that one reason so many Americans go to therapists is because they don't have any true friends they can really talk with about their problems. A third perception is that by always attempting to put a positive spin on everything, Americans create the impression with Germans that they are dreamers who don't have their feet planted firmly on the ground.

Naturally enough, whether German complaining takes place in the public sphere or among friends in the private sphere will determine what form the complaining takes. In the private sphere the complaining will be more emotional, more direct, and with less consideration for appearing reasonable. The more serious or formal a situation, the more matter-of-fact and impersonal one should be in expressing a complaint.

Nonverbal Communication

While verbal strategies and tactics comprise a major part of any communication style, the use of one's body and voice is just as important, if not more so. In general, German communication style is marked by more constrained use of both bodily and vocal resources than the American style. Thus, the private/public distinction, which is such an important dimension of German culture in general, is also very noticeable in the nonverbal communication of Germans. This can be seen in a variety of dimensions, such as smiling, physical distance, touching, and vocal quality—all of which affect the style and emotionality of any given conversation.

Vocal Quality

Generally, German voice patterns tend to be somewhat deeper and exhibit fewer modulations than do American voice patterns and are viewed by Germans as a way of remaining in control and divorcing emotions from reason.

In line with their fondness for complaining, Germans are also more willing to use their tone of voice to express negative emotions of anger, frustration, and irritation than are Americans. This tends to upset Americans, who are more accustomed to vocal patterns that are typically less monotonic and more expressive of happier and positive feelings. This quality goes hand in hand with the American penchant for offering compliments and positive feedback to their conversational partner. Germans, on the other hand, complain it is precisely this vocal quality that leads them to perceive Americans as superficial and disingenuous, claiming that American voices are *überschwenglich*, or excessively exuberant.

Silences and pauses, which make Americans uncomfortable, are longer and more common in German speech, where they can even be interpreted as a sign of harmony. German speech, unless confrontational, tends to be somewhat slower and more reflective than the American tempo, in which harmony is signaled by a smooth, uninterrupted verbal flow and where pauses cause discomfort. The slower German tempo reinforces the image of being *sachlich* and thoughtfully serious. In Germany immediate replies and "thinking out loud" are less frequent than in the United States and are interpreted as overly impulsive and lacking the appropriate seriousness. In fact several German businessmen have said that they consciously use these silences as a tactic in negotiations. Because Americans are not as comfortable with a slower tempo or longer silences, they tend to get nervous and give away bargaining points when their German counterpart becomes silent.

The German tempo can speed up significantly and get louder with more frequent interruptions during a discussion where the participants have different opinions. While discussions in the *Sie* mode tend to be less heated and more reflective, these too can get more directly confrontational than is comfortable for Americans. In the *du* mode opinions are often expressed vociferously, but from a German perspective the directness and louder vocal intensity are not seen as disruptive or abnormal. Of course, there is a fine line between a heated discussion and a fight, and while Germans are practiced in using an adversarial style, they too sometimes lose control in discussions, which then turn into arguments. Germans can also be boisterous, especially in pubs and at public fairs where alcohol is served, but in general they do not talk as loudly as Americans do. Americans are more extroverted and outgoing, while Germans are more reserved and introverted. In part this German behavior is an attempt to be modest and not attract overmuch attention, especially when in public.

Distance

Because Germans dislike spectacles and prefer to remain formal and reserved in public, they will usually wait until they are in close proximity before greeting someone on the street. Hollering or waving to catch a distant person's attention is something only younger or impolite Germans do. In fact, loud foreigners irritate the more traditional Germans, which causes considerable resentment and social tension.

In stores and in public places Germans accord one another less private space than do Americans. In other words, their personal space bubble is considerably smaller than that of Americans, and they do not consider it rude to pass very close to a stranger without acknowledging the other's presence or excusing oneself. From their perspective, this is just normal public behavior and certainly not something for which one should apologize. People are simply accustomed to having less physical space and think it normal to be in close proximity with one another. The sharing of restaurant tables with strangers is indicative of this common German habit. Rather than keeping a large physical distance as do most strangers in the United States, Germans maintain this distance psychologically by not acknowledging the other's presence and by remaining formal and aloof.

Facial Expression and Eye Contact

In Germany, someone who can't look you in the eye is generally viewed as weak in character, is not to be trusted, or is hiding something. While direct eye contact is also an American characteristic, Germans have the disconcerting habit of fixing you directly with an unwavering gaze that seems to last for a fraction of a second too long and makes many Americans uneasy. Similarly, in face-to-face conversations, Germans will look you directly in the eye while talking, something which some Americans find vaguely annoying or disconcerting. From the German point of view this is a sign of honesty and true interest in the conversation. For Americans it can seem too intense and direct. On the other hand, Germans find that Americans don't maintain eye contact long enough but rather tend to let their eyes flit back and forth in the vicinity of their conversation partner, always coming back to him or her but never staring too long.

Smiles are particularly telling. Whereas an American smile often means only that someone is being polite, friendly, or personable, a German smile more often indicates real affection and is used with far more discretion, generally only with those persons one knows and really likes. Many Germans say they really enjoy the smiles and friendliness they encounter in the United States, but if they acted that way at home, they would be sending the wrong message. After all, would you want to be continually broadcasting signals of affection to most people you meet? Affection and smiles are things Germans tend to reserve for friends and family.

Bearing and Posture

German children are still taught to sit and stand up straight, which is a sign of good character. Slouching is seen as a sign of a poor upbringing. This can be illustrated in the German word *aufrecht* (upright), which is used to describe both a person's posture and bearing as well as his or her character and integrity. The more "laid-back" and relaxed postures of Americans, especially those from the West Coast and among young people, have still not taken root in Germany. The concept of "hanging loose" may seem attractive to certain Germans, but it is definitely not widespread.

Traditionally, this upright bearing and posture were reinforced by wearing clothing that was formal. While this still holds true for the older, more traditional Germans, the younger generation has become much more informal and casual. Nonetheless, if you are not sure what to wear in a particular social situation, you are well advised to err on the side of formality.

Similarly, while traditional Germans, especially men, find touching to be embarrassing, the younger generation is much more relaxed. It has become quite fashionable to touch more as well as to kiss or hug in the French style as a greeting or way of leave-taking.

A handshake used to be a mandatory part of greeting and leave-taking in Germany. Younger Germans who have adopted the French-style greeting behavior have dropped the practice. Nonetheless, it is still considered proper in more formal situations and at work, where Germans shake hands far more frequently than do Americans. Typically, upon entering a room where a formal party or business meeting is taking place, good manners require that a person shake the hands of all present. This same ritual is repeated when leaving.

If shaking hands is common in Germany, other physical gestures and body movements are more contained. Such restraint is perceived as a sign of self-discipline and emotional control. From a German perspective, Americans often seem overly emotional, more given to expansive gestures and other body movement.

****

Most people cannot easily change their communication style, especially the nonverbal components, nor would they want to; however, simply being aware of style differences and how they are culturally determined often helps one develop a more tolerant attitude toward those differences. This tolerance alone can often decrease misunderstanding and raise the level of satisfaction for those communicating across cultures.

[1] This chapter describes a style of speech used by educated Germans throughout the FRG. While there are significant regional variations, it is important to at least be familiar with this style when communicating with Germans.

[2] Kurt Lewin, "Some Social-Psychological Differences between the United States and Germany," *Character and Personality* 4 (1936): 265–93.

[3] There are also rules as to who can "offer the *du*," as Germans like to say. In practice what this means is that a person from a higher level must propose the idea of using the *du* form to the person lower in the hierarchy.

[4] Not all the questioning of the past was voluntary. The occupying forces in the western zones had started a program of enforced denazification, which was supported by many German citizens. This denazification program resulted in a major difference of opinion between East and West Germans. While West Germans in the FRG were examining and trying to come to terms with their past (*Vergangenheitsbewältigung*), East Germans in the GDR were constrained by a government that abdicated all responsibility for Nazism. The GDR's basic argument was that they—the socialists and communists—had been the enemies and victims of the Nazis and that it was now absurd for them to identify with them or to reexamine their past. By so doing the GDR authorities essentially swept the issue under the carpet.

[5] This section does not apply to those Germans from the German Democratic Republic. Former East Germans, because of forty years under a communist dictatorship, are much less confrontational and are more reticent about expressing their opinions than are their West German cousins.

6   In fact, Foster concludes that such an ethos is common in many cultures of the world. For more on this, see George Foster, "Peasant Society and the Image of Limited Good," *American Anthropologist* 67, no. 2 (April 1965).

5

The German Social Market Economy

Like so much else about Germany, the German way of doing
business is also enigmatic. How does a country with very high
labor costs and one of the strongest union systems in the
world manage to maintain its competitiveness as a world
leader in exports? The explanation lies in Germany's culture.
Many people falsely assume that an economic system is the
sum of immutable market forces combined with inviolable
economic laws. Nothing could be further from the truth, as
Hampden-Turner and Trompenaars have so eloquently
shown.[1] In any country, economic behavior mirrors the culture and the historical forces that have shaped it. In
Germany's case, the need for order, the desire for security,
and the sense of duty and responsibility are directly reflected
in Germany's *soziale Marktwirtschaft*, or "social market
economy."

Americans, especially businesspeople, sometimes find it
hard to understand why the German economic system has
functioned so well for so long. This comes from viewing the
system from two characteristically American cultural per-
spectives. The first is the central American belief in individual freedom and a strong dislike of anything that con-
strains individual liberties. The second is the corresponding
assumption that the "invisible hand" of a deregulated free

market will most effectively organize an economy, and, consequently, anything that interferes with the operation of a free market is undesirable. As might be expected, given the Germans' desire for order and security, Germany's economy is indeed highly regulated. Nevertheless, the fact that the system has worked well is borne out not only by the high standard of living in Germany but also by its export statistics. Despite a severe lack of natural resources and a population only one-third the size of the United States, Germany often runs neck and neck with the United States in the race to be the world's largest exporter.

Germany's social market system is sometimes described as capitalism with a conscience. The real driving force behind it is its underlying ethic—a strong sense of social responsibility and a desire for consensus that, together with the market structure, work to create a pragmatic balance between economic growth and the common social good. From this perspective, the free-market style of capitalism found in the United States appears too driven by greed and selfish individualism.

Germany's underlying ethic of social responsibility is directly related to the German sense of duty, which is manifested in a company's obligation to do more than simply produce goods and services. Traditionally, American and British public companies have existed to maximize return on investment for their shareholders. As in other European countries, German public companies are expected to balance the interests of their shareholders with those of their workers and the common good of the community. This expectation of social responsibility greatly shapes the German model.

Similarly, Germans believe a modern industrial society needs a "social safety net" for citizens who lose their jobs, want to have babies, get sick, need training, and so on, and they further maintain that it is the government's responsibility to provide this protective net. While the predominant view in the United States is that ultimately responsibility for being unemployed rests with the individual, Germans tend to see the individual as caught up in powerful social and market forces that require government intervention. In this view, the state needs to regulate and organize the economy responsibly in order to protect its citizens from the vagaries of the business cycle and other economic forces. In return, Germans believe it is the citizen's duty to work hard, obey the laws, and behave in a way that will benefit society. This sense of obligation and duty, for example, generates the high turnout at German elections. In federal elections, voter participation is generally around 80 percent or higher.

The social market system is not a welfare paradise, nor is it a social wonderland; rather, it is a highly competitive market system that also incorporates ideals of social responsibility and commitment to the common good. This powerful combination results in less social conflict in Germany than in other industrialized countries. The demonstrations and strikes which are common in France occur far less frequently in Germany. Furthermore, Germany has created great wealth with relatively little poverty; there is nothing in Germany to compare with the poverty of Appalachia or the violence and crime of inner cities in the United States.

German View of Business

The social market did not develop in a vacuum; rather, it is a product of previous German experiences and beliefs. Americans tend to accord successful businesspeople high status and respect. In Germany, for various reasons, business is generally viewed more negatively. When Germans consider someone's business success, one of their first questions is "At whose cost was that success achieved?" As already mentioned, Germans operate from the assumption that all resources are limited and that if someone has managed to acquire more than his or her fair share, others will suffer as a consequence. This assumption of limited resources informs and drives many discussions in Germany. It certainly played a central role in the rise of the unions and the socialist movements in Germany during the nineteenth century; it is no coincidence that the authors of the *Communist Manifesto* were Germans. Ask most Germans for their opinion, regardless of political persuasion, and they will tell you there is something fundamentally wrong in a country where one person, such as Bill Gates, can be so incredibly rich, while others are homeless or without health insurance.

Other historical factors have also played a role in the development of the Germans' negative attitude toward business. For example, in its battle to stop the growing political power of the middle class during the nineteenth century, the aristocracy adopted a derogatory attitude toward any new wealth or power created by commerce and industry. To those educated Germans with more leftist leanings, the industrialists' support of and collaboration with the Nazis was another indicator of the shortcomings of business. Such persons point out the often overlooked fact that the first concentration camps were built to contain German union leaders, socialists, communists, and others who were considered enemies by the Nazis. The forced exploitation of both foreign and German workers during that period is a part of the past that today's Germans are trying to live down.

In addition, German industry is viewed as the major source of pollution in this densely populated country, where open space and natural resources are at a premium. Environmentalism is a strong social and political force in Germany, and industry—in particular the nuclear industry—is one of its main targets.

For all of these reasons, business does not enjoy the status and positive image that it does in the United States. Germany's industrial success has created considerable wealth, but it is still considered foolish and in bad taste to flaunt it openly. German businessmen[2] are hesitant to make too much of a public splash and are almost apologetic about their great success. In line with German cultural values, they work hard at creating an image of seriousness, respectability, and social commitment. This is especially true of the smaller and medium-sized companies.

Large Companies and the Mittelstand

In Germany a clear distinction is drawn between large corporations and what Germans call the *Mittelstand*, the medium-sized companies that are critically important to the German economy. Germany's largest companies—Volkswagen, DaimlerChrysler, BMW, BASF, Hoechst, Bayer, Krupp, and Siemens—are world-renowned brand names for cars, chemicals, machinery, and electrical and electronic equipment. While these companies are in the public eye, Germany's less visible Mittelstand accounts for half of Germany's Gross National Product (GNP) and is a major contributor to Germany's exporting and economic success.[3]

Germany's large companies all have relatively similar management and organizational styles. They are characterized by fairly rigid hierarchies and vertical organizational structures with strict chains of commands and well-defined areas of responsibility. As such they exhibit organizational structures typical of traditional large U.S. companies. In fact, American management theory and consultants have had a significant impact on German organizations since the 1950s and 1960s. Matrix structures, such as those previously introduced by General Electric, were slowly gaining acceptance in Germany by the late 1970s. Since 1990, as Germany has struggled with reunification and recession, new American management ideas have been increasingly discussed and implemented by the upper levels of German business. More recently, following Japanese and American precedents, large German corporations have worked hard at becoming leaner. Both Daimler-Benz and Siemens have downsized and closed less profitable operations. Perhaps more significantly, Daimler-

Benz initiated the merger with Chrysler to create Daimler-Chrysler, clearly an attempt by Daimler-Benz to become more of a global player.

More important still, large and small German firms are beginning to develop and make products more suited to the needs and budgets of their customers. By emulating American marketing techniques, they are adding another element to their previous engineer-driven approach, which resulted in extremely reliable and high-quality but expensive products. Because the German market is less price-sensitive than other markets, this approach worked in Germany, but it effectively priced some German goods out of various sectors of the U.S. and world markets.

While large German companies have much in common with their counterparts in U.S. companies, the Mittelstand exhibits some significant differences. One key difference is their strong desire to remain independent and unknown. Hermann Simon describes the most successful of the Mittelstand companies and their maintenance of a low profile in his book *Hidden Champions*.[4] Typically these companies are privately held and highly self-reliant. Keeping tight control of the company—often in family hands—ranks as a higher priority than simply making money, and owners are rarely interested in the rapid expansion needed to take their companies public. These companies are niche-oriented and are fierce competitors in the global market, where they often control substantial market share in their particular field. Like the larger German companies, they also tend to take a significantly longer-term strategic view than do U.S. companies.

Importance of Job Security

These Mittelstand companies also have strong ties with their local communities and a clear sense of social responsibility, particularly in providing lifetime jobs for their employees. In fact, providing jobs is not just a concern of the Mittelstand, it is an issue that most Germans agree is critical for their society. Certainly the high unemployment, hyperinflation, and severe social dislocations Germany experienced during the 1920s that led to the collapse of the Weimar Republic and the rise of the Nazis explain much of the German fear of unemployment. Correspondingly, the "hire and fire" policy typical of many American companies is viewed negatively. Rather than simply firing an employee, a traditional German strategy has been, and continues to be, to shunt incompetent employees off to areas where they can do no harm. This strong attitude toward creating and maintaining long-term employment underpins the social market ethic that places a high premium on company loyalty.

Typically, German companies first hire employees for a three- or six-month probationary period. During this time both the company and the employee are sizing each other up. If one side or the other is dissatisfied with the employment situation, the probationary period can be terminated with no negative repercussions. If both sides are satisfied at the end of the probationary period, the written work contract continues in effect, committing both sides to a long-term relationship. Traditionally, German employees have expected lifetime job security, which the company has offered in exchange for good performance from the employee as well as loyalty to the company. Recently, stresses and changes in the economic situation in Germany have made this model difficult to maintain; hence, job mobility is on the increase.

Despite rumors to the contrary, it is not impossible to fire an employee in Germany, but unfair dismissal is protected by a series of complicated regulations. Drinking on the job, excessive absenteeism, theft, fighting with other employees, industrial espionage, and other undesirable behaviors are all justifiable grounds for immediate dismissal. With proper notification, workers can also be laid off because of bad business conditions.

Managerial Approaches

German management styles vary greatly, particularly among the Mittelstand companies, where the highest executive is usually also the owner. Traditionally, competent management and good leadership were seen primarily as an attribute of personal charisma or class values and not considered something that could be taught. One result of this attitude was an elitist ethos among German leaders and business executives. Another is that most German executives are specialists in their technical or scientific fields and first learned to manage while on the job through company training programs or seminars offered by private institutions. While many German executives hold scientific or engineering doctoral degrees, few have university business training of the sort offered by American MBA programs. This has begun to change, however, and professional managers are now beginning to receive more respect and credibility in the German business community. In 1994 Jürgen Dormann's appointment as chairman of Hoechst, Germany's largest chemical company, was considered big news. Mr. Dormann has a degree in business from Harvard and was the first Hoechst chairman who did not have a scientific background.[5]

Describing German managerial style is also made difficult by the presence of two seemingly contradictory tendencies that exist side by side. On the one hand, there is a strong tendency toward hierarchy and an autocratic style. On the other, there is a clear emphasis on a more democratic approach based on consensus and cooperation. Both tendencies can be found at most levels both inside German organizations and in the external socioeconomic environments in which they operate. A German manager must learn to walk a tightrope balanced between them in order to be successful.

Autocratic Style

The autocratic managerial style is top-down and is characterized by direct orders, strong demands, and open criticism of subordinates, with little regard to notions of equality or face-saving. Autocratic managers rely on the German tradition of command and obedience, which accepts hierarchy as a given in life and which makes little attempt to disguise power differences among the ranks in the hierarchy. In the old German class system, domination of the lower by the upper classes was considered natural, and people behaved accordingly. The abuses of power during the Nazi period, however, destroyed the legitimacy of absolute obedience to authority; most Germans today are strong believers in democracy. But they are also pragmatic and see the value of a clear hierarchy in organizing society and industry. German managers and supervisors expect that subordinates will comply when direct orders are in accord with the organization's policy and the employee's job description. But from an American perspective, this direct style of communication can appear intrusive and overly brusque, if not outright demeaning.

Objective and external criteria are cited as measures of performance, and if these criteria are not met, the manager is expected to inform the employee in an explicit, impersonal manner. Because Germans separate their private and work lives so thoroughly, there is little attempt to create the illusion of equality or of friendship among various levels in the hierarchy. In fact, such attempts are often viewed as counterproductive and inefficient.

Praise of performance is rarely used to motivate employees, as is typical in the United States. Because of their thorough educational and vocational training, combined with their strong sense of accountability, Germans have internalized performance criteria and are highly self-directed. They prefer to be given a task in a clear, succinct manner and then be left alone to get on with it. The more emotional motivational strategies used by American managers are viewed as unnecessary hand-holding, and the tendency of American managers and supervisors to continually involve themselves in the work process is perceived by the well-trained German as intrusive.

Furthermore, German employees are often confused by American managers who attempt to make their criticism more palatable by prefacing it with praise for the things the employee did right. Both employees and managers take the old Swabian saying *Net g'schimpft isch Lob g'nug* (If you weren't criticized, that's praise enough) quite literally.

The German respect for rationality means that a matter-of-fact, no-nonsense approach predominates. This is especially true of the more autocratic managers who believe in the need for discipline and the strict separation of work and private life and who avoid any of the more American approaches that emphasize human relations or the breaking down of hierarchical distance. As a result, many Germans find their work environment to be highly stressful and claim that their long vacations are absolutely necessary in order for them to recuperate. As in the United States, work-related stress leads some German managers to suffer from depression and related illnesses. Significant alcohol and substance abuse among managers has also been reported.

Consensus and Cooperation

Despite the strong, traditional autocratic style of many managers, some German managers have adopted a less formal, more egalitarian style. While few Americans associate democracy with German history, such tendencies existed early on. Evidence from the earliest Germanic tribes shows a class system headed by a warrior elite.[6] As in ancient Greece, decisions among this upper class were made in assemblies, and tribal leaders were elected by the freemen of the warrior class. Each freeman had the right to voice his opinions in the tribal discussions that determined tribal policies. Although this early democratic spirit was largely lost in the subsequent absolutist domination of European politics, it is quite plausible that today's widespread use of consensus in Germany is directly related to this ancient cultural practice. Manifestations of this process are still visible in the German language, where the verb *abstimmen* (to vote or decide) is directly related to *Stimme*, the word for "voice."

This tendency reemerged at various times in German history, gaining prominence after World War II, when German employees and owners found a common cause in their need to survive and rebuild Germany. Today the German model is characterized by its attempts to maintain social peace through use of consensus and cooperation at all levels of society. Thus German politicians, union leaders, and businesspeople often join together for roundtable discussions to work out German industrial policy. In large German corporations, the CEO is generally first among equals, the managerial board atmosphere is typified by collegial working practices, and decision making (see chapter 6) by consensus is common on the different working levels of the hierarchy and within departments.

The German style of discussion described in chapter 4 is a direct outgrowth of this strong German desire for consensus. In 1992 I witnessed how this German need for consensus differs from that of the French. At that time I was a participating researcher for the *Deutsch-Französische Jugendwerk* (German-French Youth Office), which was set up to promote friendship among the youth of these two former enemies. At our semiannual meeting, our main group of about twenty researchers separated into French and German subgroups to better discuss an important issue. We had agreed to rejoin the plenary group in one hour to present our findings. After seventy-five minutes, our group of Germans was still intensely discussing the issue in order to reach some common point of view it could present to the whole group. We reluctantly broke off our discussion before reaching an agreement because we were so obviously behind schedule, but no one was happy about it. Leaving the conference room, we found small groups of French researchers sitting in various areas in the hotel and bar in relaxed conversation. They had only spent about forty-five minutes talking in their group. During that time they discovered they had very different viewpoints on the subject, at which point they all agreed to disagree, broke off their discussion, and left to find what they considered a more pleasant use of their time. Americans in the same situation would probably have discussed the pragmatic dimension of the issue and then put it to a vote!

The French lack of commitment astounded the Germans, who find it more difficult to agree to disagree. Germans take the notion of reaching consensus seriously because they believe it is necessary in order for them to cooperate and work well together. Consensus is seen as a major foundation for a stable and secure society. This emphasis on cooperation and partnership is mirrored in several important verbs beginning with the word *mit* (with) that Germans use regularly in the workplace. *Mitarbeiten* (to work together), *mitdenken* (to think along the same lines), *mitreden* (to have the right or duty to speak out), *mitwirken* (to participate in), and *mitbestimmen* (to codetermine) all illustrate the central position of consensus and social cooperation in German society.

This German style of social cooperation is very different from the Japanese version, which is based on social harmony and maintaining harmonious relationships. To outsiders, the German style often appears anything but harmonious. It encourages direct expression of conflicting viewpoints, and confrontation is generally seen as an unavoidable part of the process. While strong positions are staked out early on, ultimately the different sides are expected to reach an agreement acceptable to all parties involved. During such negotiations, Germans don't place great emphasis on face-saving tactics. Instead, they expect each participant to be able to verbally defend his or her own position in an articulate manner. Such discussions take the form of verbal dueling, and it is a sign of respect to neither give, nor expect, quarter. The same is true of German negotiators, whose motto seems to be "If you can't stand the heat, get out of the kitchen."

As in the autocratic style, the German preference for rationality clearly influences the consensus approach. In such group settings Germans emphasize maintaining the correct social distance. Shows of emotion, other than moderate irritation or anger, are considered inappropriate. This creates a more impersonal atmosphere, which is emotionally comfortable for the participants and which makes such group meetings more effective and functional for the organization.

Mitbestimmung *and* Two-Tiered Boards

The *Mitbestimmung* (codetermination) law of 1976 requires that all stock companies with over two thousand employees have a two-tiered board system. The upper board, called the *Aufsichtsrat* (supervisory board), appoints the *Vorstand* (executive or management board), which actually runs the company. The law requires that equal numbers of owners and laborers be represented on the supervisory board. While such a setup might seem like a nightmare to an American manager, it is representative of the German desire for social and economic consensus and works well in Germany. That Germany has one of the lowest rates of workdays lost to industrial strikes in Europe is a direct result of this policy.

Having workers represented directly in the boardroom has increased the trust and cooperation between labor and management. This high degree of cooperation is implicit in the term *soziale Partner* (social partners), which Germans use to describe the relationship between management and labor. Labor has an institutionalized means of input in the decision-making process. Nevertheless, the final say is left to the owner's representatives, because the chairman of the supervisory board has two votes and represents the shareholders. In the case of a tie vote, the owners are guaranteed to win. In practice, however, this tiebreaker system is rarely needed; most issues are decided unanimously or left undecided until a consensus is reached at a later time. While this lengthens the decision-making process, it is a typical example of the German desire to avoid the more adversarial labor-management relations that are typical of France and other European countries.

The Vorstand differs significantly from an American board of directors. While American boards are often dominated by a powerful CEO and subject to factionalism, the German Vorstand is characterized by a more collegial atmosphere among members who identify strongly with the company and thus work together as a team. German CEOs are well paid, but they do not receive the huge salaries American executives do. For example, one topic of discussion during the Daimler-Benz merger with Chrysler was the discrepancy between CEO salaries. While Daimler-Benz's CEO, Jürgen Schremp, is thought to have earned slightly under two million U.S. dollars, Chrysler's CEO, Robert Eaton, was reportedly earning over sixteen million dollars. In fact, wage differentials in Germany are among the lowest of the world's major economies.[7]

The board members, like most German managers and employees, also identify more strongly with their company than do American executives. While many American executives are graduates of MBA programs and are quite willing, even expected, to switch companies, and often industries, in the course of their careers, German executives, as said earlier, tend to be technical specialists and scientists who stay with one company most of their career, gradually working their way up through the ranks. Internal promotion to fill senior positions creates strong loyalty and identification with the company, which in turn strengthens and stabilizes German organizations. This loyalty, combined with a willingness to make decisions on a consensus basis, greatly helps in the implementation of difficult decisions.

Mitbestimmung and the Works Council

Mitbestimmung is also apparent in Germany's smaller companies, the Mittelstand. German law allows all companies with five or more permanent employees, not including managers, to form a *Betriebsrat* (works council). The number of workers on this council varies, depending on the size of the company. For companies with three hundred employees or more, one full-time employee must work solely on council matters. For the largest companies, as many as fifty employees sit on the works council. Some of these are full-time council members; others are regular employees who receive time off to fulfill their council duties. Councils are not simply Trojan horses for Germany's strong unions,[8] because members are directly elected by all workers, regardless of union affiliation. In fact there have been instances in which councils have sided with management against the unions.

According to law, works councils must give their consent before management can hire or fire employees, change working hours, or decide on issues of safety. Furthermore, management often consults with the council on planning issues, and the council has access to reports on the company's performance.

In some companies councils are looked upon as respected partners by management; in others they are considered a necessary evil. The works council maintains regular communication with management and is generally taken seriously. Needless to say, some German managers and politicians are not happy with this system, which gives so much power to labor. From an American manager's perspective the works council system may seem like a severe impediment to efficiency, but once the system is understood, the American can usually adapt. One CEO of an American subsidiary in Germany said the key was to establish a sound business relationship with the works council. He noted they wanted more information about the company's plans than he was used to giving in the United States, but together they had developed a good working relationship based on mutual respect and trust.

Germany's system of industrial democracy has two major advantages. First, by avoiding the more adversarial positions taken in other industrialized countries, labor and management tend to see themselves as interdependent partners. Awareness of this interdependence encourages both sides to maintain a responsible dialogue, which reduces potential conflict. Second, because labor is involved in the decision-making process earlier on, implementation of decisions, especially difficult ones, is easier. This is in stark contrast to American companies in which decisions are made at the top, after which management tries to get employees to "buy in." Because German workers have a say in the actual decision-making process, they have "bought in" from the beginning, so that while decision making takes longer in Germany, implementation can be faster and more effective.

While these advantages help achieve stability in the social market economy, the many regulations created to implement them have also resulted in an overly protected and rigid economic system.

The Apprenticeship System

German management works hard at maintaining good relationships with its employees because so much has been invested in them via the apprenticeship system.

Germany's apprenticeship system, rooted in the medieval guilds, consists today of approximately 380 core occupational training programs within a dual-track educational system. This system, a prototypical example of the cooperation between state and industry, guarantees young Germans a first-rate occupational education. For three years apprentices receive a thorough theoretical education at state vocational schools while concurrently acquiring the necessary job skills and experience in half a million German companies. The total apprenticeship program costs German industry an estimated twelve billion dollars (U.S.) annually,[9] and while this investment greatly increases Germany's labor costs, it also creates a highly trained workforce.

No company is required to offer this vocational training, but many do. Behind this system is the assumption that every job, no matter how simple, needs to be done well if the economy is to run smoothly. Apprentices learn not only the pragmatic aspects of their particular vocation but are also taught how their job fits into the larger industrial whole. They understand that doing their job poorly will have a negative effect on both their company and the economy. This training infuses them with a stronger sense of social responsibility and personal accountability.

Management theorists have been enthusiastic about quality control circles, which had such success in Japan. Although superficial examination of German companies indicates few explicit quality control procedures, Germany is, nevertheless, famous for its high-quality products. The explanation for this apparent discrepancy is the high value that Germans inherently place on Gründlichkeit, or doing something well by being thorough. This basic cultural trait is reinforced in the apprenticeship system, which in turn makes "Made in Germany" synonymous with quality.

Young Germans enter the apprenticeship program when they are around fifteen, during which time they receive a moderate wage from the company with which they are training. By age eighteen, they have finished their training and are ready to take their place in the company's workforce. Internships and on-the-job training in U.S. companies have little in common with the rigor and thoroughness of the German apprenticeship program, where hard work and diligent study are required to pass difficult practical and theoretical exams. A German manager expects to tell the worker only what is needed and to explain the project goal. Once the worker understands, the manager assumes he or she will complete the project with little supervision.

To many Americans, who are used to changing jobs regularly, the notion of picking one's lifelong occupation at such an early age is overwhelming. Germans are less bothered by this idea, preferring stability, job security, and fringe benefits over the freedom of choice to pursue a variety of jobs. Typically, Germans emphasize commitment and perseverance more than individual choice and are therefore more willing to adjust and compromise. In addition, because they typically focus more of their energies on their lives outside of work and have more vacation time and shorter working hours than do Americans, it is easier for them to accept the limitations that any given occupation may bring with it.

The German apprenticeship system trains bank clerks, painters, plumbers, mechanics, machinists, lab technicians, computer specialists, retail-sales clerks, bakers, and workers for hundreds of other occupations. In the highly competitive German market, products and services must be reliable and of the highest quality, because German consumers rarely consider a low price tag their highest priority. One of the quickest ways to fail in Germany is to produce or sell low-quality products.

Industrie und Handelskammern (IHK)

Supervision of the apprenticeship system is carried out by the *Industrie und Handelskammern* (Chambers of Industry and Commerce), which are somewhat comparable to the Chambers of Commerce in the United States. There are, however, some important differences. Like the apprenticeship system, which it carefully monitors, the IHK traces its history back to Germany's medieval guild system. As with so many other vestiges of Germany's past, the original institutions went through various phases of development. Perhaps the most formative point came when the Rhineland area of Germany was occupied by Napoleon, and the French *chambres de commerce* were established. Since then Chambers of Industry and Commerce in Germany have looked after their members' various needs while also serving as advisers to the government.

A major difference between the network of eighty-three regional chambers that together form the German Association of Chambers of Industry and Commerce and their American counterparts is that membership in the IHK is compulsory for all businesses. Unlike the American Chambers of Commerce, which are private organizations with voluntary membership, the IHK are incorporated under public law and accorded the same legal status as state bodies. As such they are self-regulating and self-financing. Currently, the IHK comprises more than three million firms, whose membership dues finance chamber activities.

Compulsory membership derives in part from the notion that public tasks and public rights apply to everyone, entrepreneurs included. This perspective incorporates the idea that the entire business community should have an organization which can both regulate itself and represent its own needs and interests within society. Services offered to members by the IHK are numerous and varied. One of its most important responsibilities is to sort through great masses of data and make relevant information available to members via counseling, educational programs, and data banks. As already mentioned, they also serve a paramount role in administering and supervising the dual-track apprenticeship program. Furthermore, they serve a lobbying function in government for the interests of German business and industry. As such they represent another important link in the tightly interwoven infrastructure of the social market economy.

The Role of Banking

Like the IHK, German banks also serve a linking and networking function in the German economy. It is difficult for Americans to conceive of the vast power of German banks or of the huge role they play in the German business environment. There are several crucial differences between German and American banks. German banks are conservative, universal financial institutions that have developed close, long-term relationships with German companies and the government. These tight relationships are crucial links in the social market economy, and they have a strong impact on the way business is done.

Unlike American banks, individual German banks can and do engage in just about every conceivable type of financial activity. The universal banking system in Germany—which is outlawed in the United States and Japan—allows a German bank to simultaneously engage in investment banking, commercial banking, merchant banking, insurance sales, funds management, and more. Because of these universal financial activities, banks are involved in almost all financial transactions that take place. Germans defend this system by claiming that their banks are generous lenders and that this wide range of financial activities allows them to provide their customers with almost any financial service they desire. This is considered important because the large majority of German companies do not go public; instead, they rely on bank loans to meet their capital needs. One result is that German managers have more autonomy and are less closely scrutinized by shareholders. In theory they are expected to use this freedom to deliver steady profits and long-term growth at low risk. In practice this is not always the case, and opponents of the system want more shareholder control to encourage better economic performance. Another result is a system that tends to leave control of companies in the hands of a relatively small number of people, creating organizations that are resistant to mergers and hostile takeovers.

Long-term relationships between banks and business have created a complex series of cross-ownership in German companies, which is visible in the overlapping directorships of supervisory boards on which many German bank representatives sit. Deutsche Bank (DB), for example, owns 25 percent of Daimler-Benz, Germany's largest corporation, and Deutsche Bank's director is the head of Daimler's supervisory board. In 1993, DB acknowledged significant holdings in twenty-five other major German companies, including Metallgesellschaft and Munich Reinsurance. According to *The Economist*, in 1991 DB held approximately 120 seats on German supervisory boards.[10] While German banks may be starting to divest their industrial holdings,[11] they are still a cornerstone of the German economy.

The executives in these tight, secretive networks are often criticized as being a clubby elite who wield too much power. Accusations of insider trading on the stock market go hand in hand with this image. Interestingly enough, until recently insider trading was not considered a criminal offense in Germany. It was only under pressure from its European Union partners that Germany agreed to make insider trading punishable by law.

Defenders of this system, however, argue that while there have been abuses of power, banks prove their worth by being loyal, long-term supporters that stand by companies when bankruptcy threatens. As proof they cite the huge bailouts of AEG-Telefunken and Metallgesellschaft by German banks. Similar loyalty was shown when Deutsche Bank led the defense of Continental Tire against Pirelli's hostile takeover bid in 1991. This last case typifies the traditional desire of the business elite to keep German businesses in German hands, another example of the strong insider/outsider distinction. While it is not unheard-of for German companies to be taken over by foreign interests, it rarely happens when the business community considers the company an important national asset.

Risk Aversion

Germany was a relative latecomer to industrialization in Europe, and there was little free capital available for investment. German banks stepped in to fill this need and began the process of developing the strong and direct links with German companies described above. German bankers and businessmen are well known for their caution and desire to avoid risk. While this conservatism is changing somewhat with younger generations, Germans are still much more averse to taking risks than are Americans overall.

This "risk-aversive" mindset is manifest in the average German's reluctance to invest in the stock market, his or her unwillingness to finance purchases with credit cards, and an almost religious devotion to saving money. Financial conservatism is also apparent in the difficulty that new companies have in finding venture capital for start-ups in Germany. Investors tend to prefer bonds over stocks, and these bonds then tend to be held longer and traded less, leading to more stable, less volatile financial markets.

This financial conservatism is deeply rooted in the traumatic experience of having their savings lost and their economy destroyed twice in this century. As a result, Germany's central bank, the *Bundesbank*, is legally charged with maintaining price stability and a low inflation rate. The fear of inflation was also at the heart of Germany's reluctance to give up its national currency in favor of the euro.

Financial conservatism and the Germans' sense of angst result in their inclination to protect themselves with every conceivable form of insurance, including not only life, auto, and home insurance but also legal insurance, theft insurance, personal liability, travel insurance, accident insurance, and more. In 1991 Germans paid out $33 billion for insurance.[12] Thus, it is no surprise that Germany is Europe's largest insurance market or that Germany's Allianz is the worlds' largest insurance company. In 1997 its investments were estimated to be worth 469.5 billion marks,[13] more than the gross national product of many small countries. As is typical of the German market, Allianz does not compete by offering the lowest prices; it emphasizes instead its reliability in processing claims.

Long-Term Relationships and Secrecy

Similarly, Germans prefer to buy insurance from a local agent they know and trust, even if he or she does not offer the lowest prices. German banks use this cultural preference for long-standing relationships to their advantage by having a wide range of contacts in the German business and political community. Such contacts constitute a major resource, which they use in advising their clients and serving them in both networking and personnel recruiting capacities. This networking function is especially important in a country that so clearly differentiates between insiders and outsiders.

Not surprisingly, Germans are inclined to do thorough background checks before they feel comfortable entering into a deal with someone new. This makes breaking into business in Germany a longer, more difficult undertaking than in the United States.

One effect of this close-knit business network in Germany is the high value placed on discretion. From an American perspective, German businesspeople often seem quite secretive, and information flow within organizations appears rather restricted. Germans consider discretion appropriate in order to protect business relationships and confidential information. Because relationships have been built over time and because they investigate one another quite thoroughly, German businesspeople know a lot about both their partners and their competitors, and they are very careful to whom they divulge information about either. Germans are quite aware that information is power, and they are rarely willing to share it.

Their bookkeeping systems provide a good example of this secretiveness. Whereas accounting procedures in the United States are relatively standardized and are subject to regular public scrutiny, the German system is much less transparent. German accounting practices allow far more freedom to companies who wish to keep their assets hidden. This is one major reason why so few German companies are listed on

American stock exchanges. In order not to divulge their financial records and make known their hidden assets, they have traditionally preferred to remain outside the American financial markets. By building up long-term relationships with German banks, they have assured both their privacy and sufficient capital to meet their investment and cash-flow needs. Daimler-Benz's 1993 decision to adopt the more transparent American accounting standards was a major event for the German business community and may have started a trend.

Long-Term Planning

Germans claim that raising capital through bank loans rather than by selling shares allows them both more control and the ability to engage in longer-range strategic planning. Business decisions need not take quarterly reports into account as in the United States, and bankers, because of their close relationship with companies, are willing to sit out more years without a profit in exchange for stable returns. Long-term planning is visible in many parts of the German business world, from strategy planning and decision-making processes to the actual construction of physical plants. This approach gives German businesses a security and stability sometimes lacking in the United States, whereas U.S. businesses are more agile and can deal more flexibly with change. The American tendency toward short-term planning upsets many Germans. For example, while chemical plants in the United States are often expected to begin making a profit within three years after start-up, German chemical plants may not reach the break-even point for five years or more. This means a greater willingness to invest more money in buildings and equipment, which are then expected to last longer. This approach is not limited to business. Walk through any of the old parts of a German town and you can perceive a sense of history. Germans expect stability and dependability in their buildings and infrastructure. It's not surprising, then, that they look for the same qualities in their business relationships.

Doing business successfully in Germany means showing the Germans that you are there for the long haul and will not pull out after making a quick profit. This long-term commitment has helped both General Motors (Opel) and Ford do well in Germany. Unfortunately, American businesspeople are often stereotyped as "sharks," who are not interested in building up a lasting relationship based on reliability and mutual dependence but are only out for a quick financial "kill."

The Role of Government in Business

The final institutional piece in the social market system is the German government. While American businesspeople prefer to limit government involvement in the economy, encouraging deregulation and restricting government intervention in the free market, Germany took a different tack. Germany was a latecomer to the Industrial Revolution, so the government took an active economic role in order to protect both the country's markets and fledgling industries as well as to ensure Germany's industrial military preparedness. Prussia in particular was interested in creating a modern army, which could only be accomplished with the help of industry. These historical forces helped create strong links between government and industry in Germany that continue to the present day. Perhaps these links are not as institutionalized or as strong as evidenced in Japan, but they are a substantial force in the German economy, and Germans find this level of government involvement normal.

Various branches and levels of the government function as mediators and power brokers in the consensus process typical within German political, social, and economic institutions. These functions range from helping avert labor-management disputes to creating industrial policy. It was in this role that Chancellor Kohl and his government developed the "solidarity pact" announced in the autumn of 1992. This pact called for a general belt-tightening in Germany in order to finance reunification and strengthen the German economy. Germans expect and comply with such government action in order to maintain economic performance and the resulting social well-being.

The *Treuhandanstalt* (Institute of Trustees), created as a temporary institution to aid privatization by selling or closing down the state-owned companies of the former German Democratic Republic, provides another example of the role of government in German business. The government's active role in directing financial and industrial policy during the integration of East and West Germany was generally considered a proper role for the government.

Because the issue of unemployment is of prime importance for Germans, government involvement can also include direct ownership of companies. For example, the federal *Land* (state) of Lower Saxony is the largest shareholder in Volkswagen, and Berlin owns several banks including Landesbank Berlin and the Berliner Bank. To the extent that such ownership provides jobs, promotes social stability, and offers good service, Germans see no cause for complaint. Winds of change are blowing throughout Germany, however, as the recent privatization of the German railway, television, post, and telecommunications systems illustrates.

Women in Business

In addition to the recent wave of privatization, the changing role of women is also shaking up German businesses. Traditionally in Germany, as in most Western countries, women were rarely employed in the world of business. World War II, however, played a major part in introducing women to the workplace. With the men in military service, plants and factories needed new laborers, and it was the women who filled this need. After the war, it was only with the help of the *Trümmerfrauen* (women of the rubble) that Germany was able to rebuild its infrastructure so quickly and successfully. The determination, perseverance, and industry of these women are legendary in Germany.

Since World War II, women have increasingly joined the workforce. In fact, women today make up a large portion of the workforce, but the percentages vary considerably between eastern and western Germany.[14]

This is not surprising, given the former East German policy that every citizen had both the right and the obligation to work. The GDR's infrastructure included an extensive system of day-care centers, which allowed women to both work and be mothers. However, following reunification, women in the east were the first to be laid off, and many of the advantages they had gained under the socialist system were lost, for example, abortion on demand. Many of these women are angry about the losses they have incurred since reunification.

A different social ethos and infrastructure existed in the states of the former BRD, or West Germany. This ethos is largely captured in the commonly heard phrase *Kinder, Küche, Kirche* (children, kitchen, church). Today this phrase is used more often in the rural areas, but there are still many older Germans who believe a woman's role is to raise children, nurture her family, and obey the older Christian dogma of women as subservient to men.

Typically (although this is changing rapidly), women have been expected to make a decision to either pursue a career or be a mother; it has often been assumed that women prefer to be mothers and that those who work often do so because they can't find a man. Those who choose both career and family are still often stigmatized as *Rabenmutter* (literally, "raven mothers"), who sacrifice their children's well-being and proper upbringing for their own selfish goals. According to this ethos, children need to have a full-time caretaker in order to grow up healthy and happy.

The West German infrastructure was built on the assumption that mothers would stay home with the children. Schools, while rigorous in academic subjects, provide few other activities for pupils; as a result, they are on their own shortly after midday and need supervision. Store hours, while they have recently been extended, are still limited, making it difficult for parents to work and do the family shopping—and lack of space and small refrigerators make regular food shopping a necessity. In addition baby-sitters and day-care centers are rare, and kindergartens, while inexpensive, are often crowded.

Because of these social patterns, the roles of mother and housewife are generally accorded more status in the former West German states than in the United States, and many women, both working-class and college-educated, have happily chosen to be full-time housewives and mothers.

There are clearly major differences in the way these issues are seen by the different generations, however. Typically, older men, but also many older women, feel threatened by women's changing roles. This is especially so now that those occupations that do not revolve around sheer muscle power are growing in importance, such as the newer service and information technology sectors. But while older German males feel their social roles and identity are being called into question, many younger German males openly welcome these changes.

Recent decades have brought many new freedoms for young women in Germany, and their increased enrollment in Gymnasium as well as admission to universities is only one sign of this change. More importantly, their self-image and self-confidence have grown, and they are less willing to be denied positions that were once considered open to men only.

But even if more and more women are entering the workforce in Germany, it is still obvious that only a few are making it into the upper echelons. Women managers are still much rarer in Germany than they are in the United States, and German women in top management are still an exotic species. Again, many older men still believe that women are simply incapable of holding such positions.

Other factors contributing to the glass ceiling for women include the absence of sexual discrimination and harassment laws in Germany and the fact that women must perform better than their male colleagues to move up the ladder or even receive the same compensation. Many German women also complain that because of old prejudices and their increased visibility, they are subject to more critical performance appraisals and control than their male peers.

Germany's lack of discrimination and sexual harassment laws stands in stark contrast to the situation in the United States, where women's rights and equal opportunity are major social issues. Certainly some German women are dissatisfied with the lack of legal protection they receive regarding discrimination, but the issue of sexual harassment is something that many Germans, both male and female, find difficult to understand. In fact, in many of my seminars I am often asked why this issue is of such great importance in the United States.

I suspect that because Germans in general tend to separate their private and public lives so completely, thus creating a more formal, impersonal atmosphere in the workplace, the issue hasn't developed the importance it has in the United States. Additionally, Germans take a more matter-of-fact, biological approach to sexuality, and this seems to create a less charged atmosphere when males and females work together. Also, traditional occupational roles in the workplace limited the interactions between men and women, but as more and younger women enter the workforce, the chance for misunderstandings and gender conflict will most likely increase.

Certainly there are many factors involved in the complex gender dynamics in the workplace, but, paradoxically, progressive German maternity leave also plays a significant role. By law, German women may work in the six weeks prior to giving birth but may not be forced to do so. If they choose not to work, they still receive their full wages and benefits. Additionally, the law forbids German women to work for the first two months after giving birth, and employers must pay them their full wages and all benefits.

Germans believe strongly in the importance of raising children as naturally as possible (e.g., breast-feeding is common and visible in public places), and to help mothers raise their children, the German legislature has instituted the *Erziehungsurlaub* (child-raising vacation). This law requires an employer to hold open a woman's position, or an equivalent one, until her child's third birthday. During this time the mother is not paid, though she is eligible for some monetary support from the government. Incidentally, either the father or mother may take Erziehungsurlaub, but fathers taking it are as rare as women in top management. Needless to say, the Erziehungsurlaub can be a major financial burden, especially for smaller companies, and many employers cite it as a reason why they would be less likely to hire a woman.

Still, as Germany moves to a more service- and information-oriented economy, companies are realizing they cannot afford to ignore the great resource that qualified German women represent. More and more companies as well as federal and state governments are implementing *Frauenförderungsprogramme* (women's promotion programs). While these programs occur more often on paper than in reality at this point, they are another sign that the role of women in German business is changing.

As women are slowly advancing upward in German businesses, so are they also gradually making inroads in the various technical professions that were once viewed as a male bastion. Some German universities are even setting up technical programs just for women. Nevertheless, women are still more commonly found in the fields they traditionally occupied: nursing, teaching, sales, hairstyling, administration, translation, and support services.

The secretarial role traditionally afforded women the most opportunity for gaining access to well-paid, responsible positions. To this day ambitious German women who are willing to work at increasing their qualifications by learning foreign languages, logistical skills, and administrative competencies can become *Chefsekretärin* (head secretary). These Chefsekretärinnen are personal secretaries to German executives and are powerful people in their own right. They are often called the *rechte Hand des Chefs* (right hand of the boss) and can be quite intimidating in their gatekeeping functions. These Chefsekretärinnen will not lose their power in the foreseeable future, and it is wise to treat them with the formality and respect they deserve and are accustomed to.

Other Changes in the German Business Environment

Since the early 1990s, fault lines have become apparent in the German model, and a heated public debate is currently in progress as to what must be done to save the economy from further decline. Clearly, times have changed, and the German model faces major challenges. Reunification is proving to be more difficult and expensive than expected. Germany's manufacturers are struggling as lower-wage producers in emerging markets enter an ever more competitive global market. Germany's engineering style worked well when the rate of change was slower, but it may prove to be less successful in a faster, more service-based information economy, where flexibility and time to market become crucial.

As recession and external competition take their toll, the government and social partners are faced with difficult decisions. Will they be able to maintain a socioeconomic system based on consensus and cooperation—which was built on high wages and a generous social security system—when money becomes tighter? Recent proposed budget cuts in this system have already raised the tension level of the ongoing debate in which two opposing viewpoints clash.

Some voices advocate more "Americanization," that is, more deregulation and less government intervention as well as breaking up the secretive, long-term relationships and patterns of cross-ownership in order to make Germany more flexible and responsive to the economic challenges the country is facing. Others argue for a strengthening of both traditional cultural values and the German model. These voices argue that too much self-serving individualism and an economy based solely on a profit motive will only bring about the great disparity in wealth and the growing underclass that are associated with so much of the poverty and crime in the United States. As Germany approaches the millennium, we can expect this debate to intensify.

[1] Hampden-Turner, Charles, and Alfons Trompenaars. *The Seven Cultures of Capitalism* (New York: Doubleday, 1993).

[2] I have intentionally chosen the masculine form of this word as it more adequately reflects the reality of German business. While this is now changing and more women are opening their own businesses, married German women generally do less work outside the home and there are fewer women represented in business and the professions than men in Germany.

[3] Philip Glouchevitch, *Juggernaut: The German Way of Business* (New York: Simon & Schuster, 1992), 57.

[4] Hermann Simon, *Hidden Champions: Lessons from 500 of the World's Best Unknown Companies* (Boston: Harvard Business School Press, 1996), 3–5.

[5] "Adored No More," *Economist*, 21 March 1998, 84.

[6] Kurt F. Reinhardt, *Germany: 2000 Years*, vol. 1 (New York: Frederick Ungar Publishing, 1966), 13.

[7] "Metall Bashing," *Economist*, 19 February 1994, 16.

[8] It will come as no surprise that in a country which sets such high store on order and organization, workers in Germany are also very well organized. Approximately 40 percent of the workforce is unionized, and German unions are large and powerful. In contrast to Britain, one union represents all workers in any particular industry and negotiates on their behalf in the collective bargaining process.

[9] Philip Glouchevitch, *Juggernaut*, 130.

[10] "New Dreams at Deutsche Bank," *Economist*, 22 June 1991, 79–80.

[11] "German Banking's Industrial Revolution," *Economist*, 19 December 1998, 106.

[12] "Saving the German Way," *Europe*, November 1992, 39–40.

[13] Allianz AG, Annual Report, 1997.

[14] Friederike Tinnappel, "Ein Potential, das Firmen langsam entdecken," *Frankfurter Rundschau*, 18 October 1996, 6.

6

Building Better Business Relationships

Cultures conceive of, use, and structure time differently. German culture is old and takes a historical approach to life, whereas the United States is newer and more future-oriented. And while these differences between the U.S. and Germany are sometimes so subtle as to be almost invisible, they significantly influence our expectations about work and business life. How important is punctuality and how long should a business dinner last? When is it appropriate to take vacation? Is it more effective to do one thing at a time, or is juggling several tasks simultaneously more preferred? How much time should be devoted to planning and negotiating sessions, and how much historical context is appropriate in a presentation? All of these questions and many more are tied together by the common thread of time, and to do business successfully in Germany, you are well served to understand their expectations in this matter.

Temporal Patterns and Punctuality

As should be clear by now, Germans are meticulous, long-term planners who value punctuality and reliability. They greatly appreciate the advantages of having a well-planned routine and are loath to let that routine be upset. For that reason, if you want to make a business contact with a German, it is wise to give yourself extra lead time to set up the appointment and to make hotel and travel arrangements. This is particularly important if your visit coincides with one of Germany's frequent trade fairs. Hosting these fairs is a major industry for German towns and cities, during which time hotel space is at a premium. While these trade fairs provide excellent opportunities to meet German businesspeople, if you wait until the last minute to make your reservation, you may find yourself without a place to stay. While last-minute reservations are often difficult, confirmed reservations are meticulously honored.

Most German companies are open for operation from 8:30 A.M. to 5:30 P.M., but many government offices, especially those open to the general public, close for the afternoon. It is also often difficult to reach someone after three on Friday afternoons, because many companies close early.

As in many parts of Europe, business slows down during the summer vacation period. Vacation periods run parallel to school vacations, which are staggered among the federal states to avoid congestion on the highways. Check each state for exact dates but count on business contacts being more difficult from mid-July until the end of August. Similarly, work slows considerably during the Christmas–New Year period, when many offices are closed. Germans also celebrate a number of other holidays, of which they make full use. Because many holidays are religious in nature, they vary depending on whether the particular state is predominantly Catholic or Protestant.

Cold calls to set up an appointment are frowned upon and rarely get a positive response. A more productive approach is to send a well-written letter—formality is crucial and a poorly written letter will work against you—and then follow up with a phone call some time later. This will help create the desired image that you are well organized, and it allows your German counterpart time to comfortably fit you into his or her schedule.

Similarly, remember that Germans take more time and need more information to reach a business decision than you generally encounter in the United States. They don't feel comfortable making hasty decisions, and they need more time to reflect and plan than most American businesspeople do. Also expect leases and contracts to run for longer periods than is typical in the U.S.

Being on time for meetings and social events is definitely the norm in Germany and is seen as a sign of respect. Arriving even a few minutes late without a good excuse is viewed as a sign of poor organization at best and as a character flaw if it is habitual. The penchant some Americans have for coming late to meetings or leaving early to create the impression of being extremely busy or very important simply does not fly in Germany. A word to the wise: don't try to fit as many appointments and invitations into your day as possible, but allow some breathing time in between. This will allow you to reach your destination with time to spare, and, more important, it will create a good impression. Germans often allow extra time to arrive at an event and then circle the block, like a plane in a holding pattern, waiting for the specified time in order to arrive exactly "on the dot," and they expect the same of you.

Business Entertaining

While business meetings often start quite early in the morning, most business entertaining is done at lunch or dinner. The "power breakfasts" that have become popular in the United States have not really caught on in Germany. Lunches usually start around noon or 12:30 and will rarely last longer than ninety minutes. Dinners will begin between six and seven and generally not end before ten, and even later on weekends, but they rarely start as late or last as long as those in Italy, France, or Spain. Punctuality is also expected for business entertaining. If your host asks you to arrive at seven o'clock for dinner, you can be sure that the other guests will be there at that time and that dinner will start shortly thereafter. If you must be late, call and let your host know in advance.

For the most part, however, business entertaining takes place in the company canteen[1] or at a fine restaurant and does not include spouses. Because of the strong distinction between their private and public lives, Germans rarely do business entertaining in private homes. However, consider an invitation to a German home an honor, because that is exactly what it is. You can expect that your host will have gone to a great deal of trouble to make the event special. The house will, of course, be clean and orderly, and the host and other guests will be dressed slightly more formally than Americans would be in a similar situation. If the host has children, they may well be at the grandparents for the evening, so you will do well to check in advance to see if it is appropriate to bring your own children. The dinner menu will be special, and the table will probably be set with the host's best silverware and china. Bringing flowers is considered appropriate; German florists specialize in creating bouquets for such occasions.

Seating arrangements, particularly at restaurants and other business social events, generally depend upon hierarchy. It is not appropriate to take a seat before the host or senior person present suggests one should do so. Similarly, it is considered rude to begin drinking before the host, who may offer a short toast. When Germans offer a toast, they make a point of looking one another in the eye, drinking, and then lowering the glass slightly before finally setting it carefully on the table.

Although more and more Germans are giving up smoking, the habit is still more common in Germany than in the United States, and many restaurants do not have separate sections for nonsmokers. Large companies now frequently prohibit smoking during company meetings, but this is not true for all firms. If you are a sensitive nonsmoker, prepare to have your limits tested while in Germany.

If the dinner was a success and the atmosphere positive, Germans will generally spend a longer time after dinner doing what they love best, engaging in Unterhaltung, which includes animated conversation as well as cultivated, critical discussion about a wide variety of topics. As explained in chapter 4, Germans are rarely at ease with small talk and prefer deeper, more profound and engaging topics, often including music, philosophy, theater, the arts, current events, and politics. Remember that not only have most German managers and executives learned at least one foreign language, they and their families come from a culture that expects them to be up-to-date on political and current events as well as to be able to hold an educated conversation on a wide variety of topics. An informed opinion and the ability to discuss such topics intelligently can help you overcome the stereotype Germans have of the "typically ignorant or naive American" and serve you well in helping develop a good business relationship. To be thought of as someone who is only interested in business and who can't talk about anything else in an articulate and knowledgeable manner will definitely be to your disadvantage.

Formality and Respect

In both business meetings and business socializing, it is important to maintain the appropriate degree of formality. One should be neither overly friendly nor too pushy. Titles and last names should always be used, and this may well remain so during the entire business operation. This is not a sign that negotiations are not proceeding well; it is simply the norm in German business. At the executive level of business, educational titles are a vestige of the old class system, where proper manners and the right background are a must. By all means, do not try to use first names unless your German host or counterpart first suggests doing so, and be aware that most older Germans will rarely suggest it.

Americans like to reduce the level of formality rather quickly as a way of indicating that a relaxed atmosphere has been created in which the participants feel at home. In the United States this relaxed atmosphere is often signaled by open office doors; use of first names; chatting and relaxed small talk about unimportant matters; an expression of enthusiasm and other emotions; the loosening of one's tie or the removal of one's jacket; and relaxed postures, including "lounging" and leaning back with hands behind the head. All of these are common signals that business is proceeding well and that a relaxed atmosphere has been achieved.

In Germany, all of the above signals carry a different, often negative, message. In particular, older and upper-class Germans tend to strongly emphasize formality and display manners that may seem old-fashioned to Americans. Thus it is not uncommon for Germans to allow the person who is oldest or has the highest rank to enter a room first or to dominate a conversation. Similarly, when introducing a younger and an older German, it is proper to introduce the younger person first. Many traditional German men will still rise when a lady enters the room and may also enter restaurants and bars first, presumably to make sure it is safe for the woman to enter, another vestige from a chivalrous past.

In summary, formality must simply be expected and accepted in Germany. It signals respect and acknowledges the other person's social status. To be effective, Americans will do well to follow along, avoiding their tendency to erase or smooth over status differences.

Status and Materialism

In the United States shows of status are preeminently material; in other words, possession of money and the things that money can buy are the signs that someone is important. Social scientists speculate that this visible emphasis on material success originates in the American ideology of an egalitarian, classless society, where each individual has an equal opportunity to work his or her way to the top, that is, the "American Dream." Reinforcing this ideology was the Protestant ethic[2] of many early Americans, who believed that God showers material success on those who work hard and are successful at what they do. While these ideas have evolved and changed over the centuries, they are cornerstones of the American mindset.

In Germany, material success is also seen as valuable and desirable, but it doesn't play the role of primary carrier of social status. Rather one's family and *Erziehung* (one's upbringing, manners, and education) account for more status than money alone, especially in the upper echelons of German society and business.

To the degree that status is manifested in material possessions, the German emphasis is on quality expressed with reserve and grace. Gaudy, ostentatious expressions of wealth and flashy, eye-catching clothing styles are generally considered bad taste. This difference can be seen clearly in styles of business dress. Whereas American businesspeople tend to stock their wardrobes with many reasonably priced garments, which offer them a wider choice of what to wear, Germans buy fewer but more expensive and conservative clothes, the quality and style of the clothes outweighing variety.

Perhaps the most important sign of ingroup status in the German business world is good manners. One is expected to know how to behave correctly in public; not to do so is *sich zu blamieren* (to cause one's disgrace), something that Germans are very anxious to avoid. Good manners are part of a child's upbringing, and because they are laid out for all to know and conform to, manners also provide a sense of security. This strong emphasis on formal manners differs from the more informal approach of Americans, who feel that comfort and the ability to converse with ease are stronger criteria for social behavior than formal social dictates. The German emphasis on formality also restricts idiosyncratic shows of personality and reliance on "people skills," which Americans use to gain rapport, create empathy, and make other people feel important and well liked. Understanding this underlying difference will go a long way in helping business relationships develop smoothly. For a detailed description of particular German manners and customs, see Susan Stern's *These Strange German Ways*, listed in the References.

Attitudes toward Work

German culture is what anthropologist Edward T. Hall labels as being strongly monochronic. This means that Germans like to do one thing at a time and tend to keep different tasks quite separate, another example of the compartmentalization described in chapter 3. What this means in the workplace is that when Germans[3] come to work, that is what they do. Their monochronic approach to work, their strict separation of business from social functions, and their strong sense of duty all combine to make traditional Germans highly productive, goal-oriented workers.

This is particularly true of the older generation, the Nachkriegsgeneration, the generation who lived through and were shaped by the harsh period directly following World War II. They look back very proudly on their perseverance and determination in rebuilding Germany from the ruins of the war and the creation of the economic miracle. For these older Germans, hard work and sheer determination were their only chance for survival.

Younger Germans have a decidedly more relaxed attitude toward work. Having enjoyed the security and material prosperity that resulted from the hard work of the older generation, these young people are more demanding and less willing to make the types of sacrifices their elders did. Today, Germans work fewer hours per week than any other industrialized country, and they will candidly tell you that the six weeks of paid vacation they receive is a basic right, not a privilege. As justification for this liberal vacation policy, they point out how high German industrial productivity is, arguing persuasively that when they are at work, they do indeed work quite effectively and with great focus.

But when the workday is finished, so are the workers. Punctuality is apparent not only in starting times but also at the end of the workday; employees see overtime as an infringement on their private lives. Many American managers have had difficulty trying to get their German employees to work overtime. In fact, the strategy of staying late to "impress the boss" has often backfired in Germany. From their boss's perspective, having to stay late to finish a job may seem evidence of poor planning and bad organization. Perhaps because Americans are less protected by a social security net, or perhaps because they socialize more on the job and work less intensely, they are generally less vocal when asked to put in unpaid overtime, often staying until the job is done.

Problem Solving, Decision Making, and Project Implementation

When Germans and Americans work together, misunderstandings and conflict can arise because of differences in decision-making and problem-solving strategies. According to Sylvia Schroll-Machl,[4] while in most respects German and American teams function similarly, certain aspects of decision making and problem solving receive different emphasis, leading to slightly different procedures and tactics. Unless carefully observed and adapted to, these subtle differences can have negative consequences when Americans and Germans are working together in bicultural teams.

According to Schroll-Machl, the German problem-solving process begins by first having members of the team assemble data and facts regarding a problem or proposed project and then discussing *relevant* issues in great detail in order to *clearly* understand the nature of the topic at hand, in particular its *Kern* (essence or core). Such discussions follow the norms and rules for Diskussion as described in chapter 4. While American teams proceed similarly, what is considered "relevant" or sufficiently "clear" varies culturally, and as we have noted earlier, Germans show a greater need for more detailed information and discussion than do Americans at this stage.

The German tendency is to see the decision-making or problem-solving process from an engineering point of view, and there is often an attempt to consider at the very outset of a project all potential problems that might arise in order to achieve the most elegant solution. No detail should be left out, and nothing should be left to chance.

Germans, in their attempts to clearly and comprehensively define and understand all potential problems, spend considerable time in long, involved, and often theoretical discussions which Americans find trying. Germans find these discussions absolutely necessary. The emphasis is *initially* far more on what the problem is, how it came to be, and what its components are and less on the final solution. Achieving a clear and thorough understanding of the problem alleviates anxiety and uncertainty and provides the more cautious Germans with the sense of security and control they prefer. It also allows them to develop a contingency plan that takes all eventualities into consideration. American corporate decision-making and problem-solving processes, often market-driven, are more open-ended in their definition of how to achieve a desired future goal or vision. Americans often start out with a short brainstorming session to define the final goal or vision and then devise a series of approximate steps to use to reach that goal before they begin working toward it. From their more action-oriented perspective, the long initial discussions of the Germans are seen as a waste of time, a sort of "paralysis through analysis," particularly because Americans assume that some plans will need to be changed and others improvised along the way. The Germans, on the other hand, say that Americans tend to act without understanding a problem, which they pejoratively call "actionism." Germans characterize this mindset as the "cowboy mentality": shoot first and ask questions later. Americans, of course, think that their approach is more efficient and creative. They think the German "stick-to-the-plan" approach leads to getting locked in to an overly rigid scheme that doesn't allow for the needed flexibility that a changing world and business environment require. Americans prefer a more open, flexible style that allows them to "keep their options open," "go with the flow," and "roll with the punches."

During the initial discussion phase, whether the focus be problem solving or project planning and implementation, all members of the German team are expected to participate and share their relevant experiences and knowledge with the group. These discussions, as we've said, involve the exchange of a great amount of detailed knowledge. Because they are impatient with such long, drawn-out discussions, Americans often do not speak up at this stage, hoping to speed up the process and finally "get to work." For the Germans, these discussions *are* an intrinsic part of the work and function as a way for the group to reach a consensus, which then will allow a far more rapid implementation of the solution they have agreed upon.

Following the discussion and decision-making phase, German team members are then able to go off and work relatively independently on their tasks, while the Americans expect more group meetings and more informal communication among individual team members to continue throughout the whole process.

One cause for this communication difference may be the

fact that employees in the United States are often given tasks for which they have little formal training. Because they may be "learning by doing," they need to communicate more with both their manager and other team members in order to do their job well and to stay coordinated with the team. Germans, because of their more thorough practical and theoretical training, seem able to work more autonomously than their American counterparts and to need less communication with other team members outside of meetings. The plan agreed to by all members of the team serves as the basis for the German team members to divide up the work as best fits their skills and qualifications and then get to work on their individual tasks. This ability to work autonomously is reinforced by a large number of written technical rules, standards, company norms, project procedures, and so on, which employees are expected to know and follow.

Another aspect of this difference in the degree of communication expected outside formal meetings may be that traditional German companies are more rigidly structured. This structuring by organizational chart and strict hierarchy tends to make German companies more compartmentalized than U.S. companies, which incorporate more informal networking among employees from different functions and hierarchical levels, creating a different mentality vis-á-vis communication practices.

The German tendency to communicate less outside of formal meetings is also reinforced by their assumption that decisions made at group meetings are binding. Americans tend to see such decisions as guidelines to be followed but that may change if the need arises or if a better solution presents itself. The fact that Americans expect such changes and improvisations to occur also discourages them from such detailed initial analysis in earlier meetings, a "We'll cross that bridge when we come to it" attitude. Again, these differences are not black and white but shades in degree and emphasis.

Presumably, too, the tendency for Americans to share more

of their personality with their coworkers, while Germans maintain a more impersonal, "work only" relationship with their colleagues, also reinforces communication differences between Germans and Americans working in teams together. The Schroll-Machl study cites the typical complaint on the part of Americans that Germans are not open to conversing about aspects of a project outside of formal settings. Germans, for their part, complain about Americans asking them redundant questions about issues which, from the German view, had already been discussed and decided in previous meetings.

The German and American styles offer the opportunity for important synergies if combined in a conscious and intentional manner. Perhaps the initial achievements of NASA provide the prime example of what level of success a collaboration between the German and American styles can achieve. After Wernher von Braun and his team of German scientists began working with their American counterparts, they developed one of the most successful scientific programs of this century, proving that such collaborations can offer brilliant results. However, because of lack of cultural awareness, such projects often go awry, causing loss of profits and resources as well as bruised egos. Such lack of cultural awareness can also cause serious misunderstandings in other arenas of business.

Negotiations

Just as there are subtle but important distinctions between German and U.S. problem-solving, decision-making, and teamwork practices, some important differences in negotiation styles also exist. Perhaps the most basic difference is the German concept of "fair price."

The notion of fair price has a long history in Europe, dating back to the Middle Ages.[5] At that time, Europeans had a different system of ethics regarding money than is currently the case. Politics, religion, and ethics were thoroughly interwoven and influenced one another. One result was that the charging of interest for lending money was considered a sin and forbidden by the Catholic church. Another assumption was that all goods and services had a fair price, and to sell above that price was unethical. This is not to say that some did not charge "what the market would bear," but such practice was considered unscrupulous and frowned upon by most.

With the coming of the Reformation and the growth of capitalist society, the idea of a fair price became marginalized but did not die out completely. This idea, in fact, still appears to influence negotiations in Germany, and it is not uncommon to hear Germans complain about overpricing as "*unverschämt teurer*" (shamelessly expensive).

Given this background, it is easier to understand German negotiation tactics. In general, Germans are tough negotiators, but they tend to be relatively straightforward. Their typical strategy is to carefully estimate the total expected costs for a given product or service and then add a reasonable percentage to that figure as profit. This is then the figure they will ask for in a negotiating session, the fair price. Because they have carefully estimated their costs, they will have well-grounded and rational arguments for how they arrived at a particular figure. And they will use these arguments to avoid making concessions. Because they have not, to their point of view, started with an unreasonably high figure, they are loath to make significant reductions in their offered price, which explains at least in part why they are considered hard bargainers.[6]

Because Americans are more likely to work from a "what the market will bear" mentality, they often include a wider profit margin and ask for an initially higher price but will make significant concessions if necessary. This sometimes makes the American negotiation style seem more *sportiv* (gamelike) and speculative to the Germans.

It is worth noting that in general Germans seem less likely than Americans to see economic issues as being "just business" or based only on natural laws of supply and demand. Their history and the framework of the social market economy encourage them to see economic issues as being directly coupled with ethical issues, and they tend to perceive charging what the market will bear as greedy and unethical. Similarly, when a German negotiator says "This is my last word," it generally is; it is not a negotiating tactic. For this reason, Germans often express irritation when the other party continues to try to negotiate. As one informant told me, in such a situation *"Sie fühlen sich in Ihre Ehre gekränkt"* ("You feel your honor has been questioned"). It is wise to remember that behind the German norm of remaining impersonal and businesslike, notions of ethics and honor play important roles. As was mentioned earlier, in Germany your word is considered your honor and not something to be toyed with lightly.[7]

Another common American practice that can be offensive to the Germans is bringing in lawyers too early in the negotiations. While it is common in the United States to include lawyers from the outset, this is not so in Germany. Traditionally, German business partners conducted all but the most complicated negotiations without involving lawyers. Only after all details had been thoroughly worked out to both parties' satisfaction were lawyers brought in to finalize the deal in the form of a contract. Because oral contracts are legally binding in Germany, this practice is still common, although as products, services, and joint ventures become more complicated or expensive, lawyers are now coming into the process at ever earlier stages. Nonetheless, be aware that including lawyers in the discussion too early can send a message of mistrust to the German who expects to be dealing only with his or her counterpart. It is best to take one's cue from the Germans.

Making Effective Presentations

As in the decision-making process, the key focus of German business presentations is often objectively defining and elaborating on the core of a problem or issue. Americans who try to convince Germans with enthusiastic, visionary presentations with lots of "bells and whistles" of the sort common in the United States are destined for a rough ride with little chance of achieving the reaction they desire.

To make an effective presentation in Germany, it is absolutely essential that Americans demonstrate that they have done their homework and that they completely understand the issue or subject. When dealing with a problem, this means showing that they understand not only the problem as it presents itself but also the context of the problem and, if possible, the history of its development. This emphasis on the more historical aspects of the subject is of great interest to Germans, and Americans can expect a series of questions on this aspect if they haven't included it in their presentation. After showing that they have indeed quite thoroughly understood the problem as well as its background, the presenters should then make an argument for the proposed solution to the problem, explaining why that particular solution appears most appropriate.

Typically, many American presenters postulate an idea or vision that is "guaranteed to be a future success." This emphasis on the future success and the brilliance of the idea often goes astray with a German audience for several reasons.

First, as we've already said, Germans abhor hype and exaggeration, and they find extroverted shows of enthusiasm überschwenglich (excessive). They prefer a more matter-of-fact style with a strong emphasis on content. Thus a German presenter will attempt to demonstrate that he or she is a well-trained specialist in the field who has considered all the aspects of an issue, in particular its risks. Germans will rarely try to create the impression that they have a vision guaranteed to be a great success, nor will they attempt to persuade their audience by a show of emotional conviction.

Second, because Germans are not native speakers of English, there will surely be several members of the audience who are struggling to understand what the presenter is saying. For this reason, a high-powered style, peppered with metaphors and idioms, will only accentuate the confusion, possibly turning the audience off even more. Audience response depends on whether the Germans feel there is real substance to a presentation or whether it is mere fluff. The criteria here will again be how thoroughly the issue was analyzed and whether the wealth of details and facts that a German audience expects are present. Americans presenting to German audiences should also be aware that critical questions from the audience are often signs of respect and interest and do not necessarily mean that the Germans were not impressed or are attacking the presenter. As in discussions, Germans like to critically compare and contrast issues with presenters as well. It is important to stay relaxed and calm, to avoid becoming defensive, and to answer the questions in a matter-of-fact way. Efficiency, performance, and quality should always be emphasized. These are important criteria for the technically astute German business audience.

Transparencies, handouts, or other audiovisual materials should be carefully checked for veracity as well as typos or other errors. Germans are perfectionists and they dot their i's and cross their t's. They also examine all printed materials carefully. Errors they find will elicit a negative reaction, and they will tend to conclude that a mistake in such materials is indicative of slipshod work and poor quality in all services and products.

Much of the desired impression on a German audience can be achieved by a German style of composure. In business situations in general, and presentations in particular, Germans try to appear calm, firm, and in control, a manner they sometimes refer to as *bestimmt auftreten*. This aura of self-confidence is characterized by one's bearing as well as one's style of speaking. Many Americans will perceive this as a commanding, military bearing, and this is not far from the truth. Posture is a major component of this style, and the German businessman will carry himself in an upright and contained way. Slouching is seen as indicative of poor character and is avoided.

If the number attending the presentation is small, say up to six or eight people, it is customary to shake hands with all present when entering the room. This ritual is also repeated upon leave-taking. By the way, many Germans still consider talking with your hands in your pockets to be bad manners.

Voice is a major factor in creating an impression, one where some Americans are at a disadvantage. German men tend to speak in a deep voice, with a guttural resonance, obtained in the back of the throat. This deeper voice and more guttural resonance create a masculine impression, which is strengthened by a shorter pitch range. This can sound monotonal to the American, but it emphasizes the matter-of-fact, no-nonsense approach that Germans appreciate. German women, too, tend to have deeper voices than their American counterparts. It is American men with higher voices who may make the weakest impression, particularly if their voice rises in pitch when enthusiastic.

Eye contact is direct and maintained while talking to someone. During a presentation, eye contact will depend on the size of the audience, but the German speaker will try to keep eye contact with at least the portion of the audience that is closest.

Along with posture, voice, and eye contact, it is wise to remember that Germans consider smiling an expression of affection and therefore inappropriate for most business situations. Like humor, smiling is best left to the private sphere or until you get to know your German counterpart quite well. Remember the impression Germans appreciate in business is one of seriousness and reliability. Humor and too much emotional coloring of one's speech or manner detract from this seriousness.

As should be clear by now, the central cultural themes detailed in chapter 3 pervade and inform the German way of doing business. But as was already mentioned, the German model is under great pressure to change. As will be shown in the final chapter, German culture in general is also under pressure and is going through a major transition.

---

[1] Most larger companies have several canteens; for example, one for the regular employees, one for midlevel management, and one for senior executives and visiting VIPs. If a German says that he is inviting you, this implies that he will pay and it would be insulting for you to insist on paying. If nothing is said, then each may pay separately, though generally the visitor trying to make a sale or contact picks up the tab.

[2] This is perhaps most striking in the Calvinist ideology of *certitudo salutis*, the notion that material success was a sign one would be accepted into the Kingdom of Heaven after death. See Max Weber, *The Protestant Ethic and the Spirit of Capitalism* (London: George Allen & Unwin, 1976).

[3] This is a major difference between former East and West Germans. While West Germans work hard at maintaining the private/public distinction at work, the former East Germans were much more relationship-oriented toward their coworkers. As a result the workplace was a major social locus in East Germany, both during and after work.

[4] Sylvia Schroll-Machl, "Die Zusammenarbeit in internationalen Teams—Eine interkulturelle Herausforderung dargestellt am Beispiel USA-Deutschland," in *Internationales Change Management*, edited by Jörg M. Scholz (Stuttgart: Schäffer-Poeschel Verlag, 1995).

[5] See Max Weber, *The Protestant Ethic and the Spirit of Capitalism* (London: George Allen & Unwin, 1976).

6   Another reason for their reputation as tough negotiators relates to time—they typically expect negotiations to be long, drawn-out affairs requiring, as they like to say, *Sitzfleisch* (a tough butt). Thus, they tend to be very patient and are often willing to wait the other side out.

7   This is especially true regarding delivery dates, which are very important for Germans. Because reliability and commitment are such important parts of the German mindset, it is never wise to promise delivery dates or other specifications that cannot be met. More to the point, Germans are careful in formulating what they are offering or commiting to, and they expect others to follow the same strict standards. Firms that make commitments they cannot keep quickly gain a bad reputation, and repeat orders are highly unlikely.

7

Wertewandel:
Creation of a New German Identity?

As Germany enters the twenty-first century, great transformations are occurring in its society and culture. Germans typically refer to these as the Wertewandel (changing of values), but it is really more than values that are changing. Many of the changes are occurring in the context of politics and economics, while others are more sociological and psychological in nature, but all affect the values and norms that Germans hold dear. In effect, Germany is in the process of reinventing itself. This final chapter looks at the most important of these changes and describes their impact on the people and their culture.

The federal elections held in September 1998 were a watershed event in postwar German history. For the first time since the Federal Republic was founded in 1949, a German government was voted out of office by the electorate. Previously, all changes of government occurred as the result of a vote of no confidence within the German parliament. In this last federal election of 1998, the electorate voted the CDU (Christian Democratic Union)/CSU (Christian Social Union)/FDP (Free Democratic Party) coalition out of office after sixteen years of governing Germany. Not only was this a clear sign that democracy is both stable and deeply embedded in the Federal Republic, it was also the first time that the newer, more progressive Green Party participated in forming the governing coalition at the federal level.

At the same time that this new, less conservative coalition (SPD and the Greens) came into power, Germany moved its political capital from Bonn eastward to Berlin. This move, which began in the spring and summer of 1999, signaled a clear shift in German perspective and national consciousness, furthering the sense of closure to the division of Germany by the occupying Allied forces. At the same time, this movement of the capital symbolizes the shift in Germany's center of gravity, strengthening its traditional economic and cultural ties with Central and Eastern Europe. While all the countries of Europe were affected by the end of the Cold War, Germany was one of the most transformed. The collapse of the Iron Curtain both ended Germany's sense of isolation as a buffer zone to the communist east and gave its citizens a new sense of openness. Germany regained the freedom that comes with having open borders in all directions, while also being able to take up its traditional place as a major player in the center of Europe. Perhaps most important, it gave many Germans the sense that they were becoming a normal country once again.

The move to Berlin is also a clear indication that the process of reunification in Germany is proceeding smoothly. Between 1990 and 1999, Germany transferred a total of about $625 billion to the territories of former East Germany and continues to transfer about 140 billion German marks (71.6 billion euros) to the east each year.[1] These funds are used for rebuilding the infrastructure, subsidizing social programs, and reducing the unemployment that still plagues the former east. As these programs continue, the east will eventually catch up with, and perhaps even surpass, the economy of the western parts of Germany. Currently the unemployment and economic problems in the east are among the strongest forces in

keeping the Party of Democratic Socialism (PDS), the suc-
cessor to the former East German Communist Party, alive
and well in the eastern states.[2] As these problems are solved,
the drain on the finances of the western states will recede,
allowing the government a freer hand in its duties.

Germany in the European Union

All of these internal changes are proceeding within the wider
context of the evolving European Union. What started out as
a small trading association among six European nations in
the 1950s has become a major force within the overall scheme
of global politics and economics. Now composed of fifteen
major European nations and destined to become even larger,
the EU has created a legal framework for the cooperation of
these nations in various political and social contexts. In
effect, these nations are now members of a unified market of
about 340 million Europeans. The most recent move by most
members of the EU to give up their national currencies in
favor of a single European currency, the euro, is of historic
importance and a major psychological leap for the Germans.

After World War II the Germans charged their federal
bank, the Bundesbank, with responsibility for the creation
and maintenance of a stable currency. After the traumatic
experiences earlier in this century with currency devalua-
tion, the creation of a stable currency was as much an emotional issue as it was a financial one. While their guilt has
kept many Germans from celebrating their national identity,
the remarkable resiliency of Germany's economy and the
strength of the German mark have been a source of great
pride and security. So, Germans' reluctance to give up their
mark for the unknown euro was not surprising. While the
debate around this issue was loud and emotional, the step
forward is another symbol of both the healing of Europe and
the creation of a new German identity.

The continuing growth of the European Union and the

process of European integration it engenders are increasing the contact of Germans with members of other cultures at many levels. As the countries of Europe grow together, they are having a strong influence on each other. With a common currency, the further opening of national borders, and the relaxation of other barriers, this process will continue to exert great influence on the Germans, most of whom are strong believers in the need for the European Union.

Multiculturalism

Germany is also being strongly influenced by the European Union's Schengen Agreement, which continues to break down national borders among European states. Today it is possible to drive between various European Union countries without having to stop at border checkpoints. This is only one aspect of increasing integration in the Union for purposes of business, work, study, and pleasure. This cross-border movement is just one factor in the development of Germany as a multicultural nation.

While the previous government did little to deal with Germany's increasing heterogeneity, one of the first important legislative measures to be introduced by the new Social Democratic Party and the Green Party coalition is designed to allow inhabitants of Germany to acquire dual citizenship. This highly controversial topic is being decided as this book is being written, and it serves to illustrate the growing issue of ethnic and cultural diversity in Germany.

Current German law, dating back to 1913, grants citizenship according to bloodline. Those persons laying claim to a German bloodline are granted citizenship relatively easily, while those residents from other ethnic lines typically find it difficult to attain German citizenship, even if they were born in Germany. What this means is that East Europeans descended from Germans have been able to attain German citizenship even though they often cannot speak the language and know little of the country. Other "foreigners," such as the 2.1 million Turks,[3] many of whom were born in Germany, have been denied citizenship.

Significant numbers of these are Gastarbeiter (guest workers), people who first arrived in Germany during the 1950s and 1960s to fill unskilled positions in the expanding German economy during the "economic miracle." These guest workers came from Italy, Turkey, Greece, and other countries with lower labor costs and higher unemployment. Originally, it was assumed these guest workers would eventually return to their home countries, but many stayed and raised their families in Germany. Today, there are millions of guest workers and their dependents and descendants living in Germany.

Many of the younger descendants, representing the second and even third generation and having grown up in Germany, typically speak excellent German and identify more with Germany than with their families' cultures of origin. The largest and least integrated group of guest workers are the Turks. Because Turks are both darker-skinned and Muslim, conservative Germans are largely against granting them citizenship. If the proposed legislation is passed, these Turkish residents would be allowed both German and Turkish citizenship, thus allowing them to become more integrated members of German society.

A second factor contributing to Germany's increasing heterogeneity is its policy toward refugees. Because its postwar political asylum policy was one of the most liberal in the world, Germany has accepted a large number of political refugees and those seeking political asylum from various countries in the world. This liberal asylum policy was yet another way Germany went about trying to atone for its past; few countries have taken in as many refugees as Germany has. But in recent years, the floods of people seeking asylum created significant financial and social strains, especially as the changes in Eastern Europe (in particular the conflict in the former Yugoslavia) caused millions of people to flee.

Because of the already-high population density, the growing economic costs of reunification, and persistent unemployment, the German parliament amended the constitution in 1993 to restrict the number of those granted political asylum.

Other factors contributing to the changing face of ethnicity in Germany are the many foreign students who come to study and then stay as well as the foreign military forces that have been in Germany since the end of the war. Even the ethnic Germans arriving from eastern European countries (Russia, Romania, etc.) are upsetting the previous homogeneity of Germany. Many of these people, descendants of Germans who left the German-speaking areas of Central Europe centuries ago and are now returning, speak an unusual dialect of German, if they speak the language at all.

This growing contact with non-Germans and the changes in ideas and behaviors that accompany this contact are slowly transforming Germany. For example, the traditional German greeting, shaking hands, has become less common among younger Germans, who now commonly follow the Latin custom of greeting with a quick kiss on the cheek. Another manifestation of this trend is the large number of foreign restaurants which can be found in most German towns and cities.

The strong predisposition of Germans to travel to all points on the globe is also increasing contacts with non-Germans. Their high standard of living and lengthy paid vacation greatly reinforce their Wanderlust. In the same vein, an increasing number of young Germans have opted to take part in study abroad programs provided by high schools and universities. After a significant period of time spent abroad, they often return to their home country with broader, more open-minded attitudes.

These are the factors that have combined to transform Germany into a multicultural society, though many Germans refuse to recognize this fact. The current debate as to whether Germany should strive to retain what remains of its ethnic homogeneity or continue its current trend toward multiculturalism is complicated and controversial. Right-wing extremists and more conservative Germans fear multiculturalism is responsible for rising unemployment and crime rates as well as a loss of core German values and norms. Younger and more progressive Germans are more welcoming of these changes, seeing in them the opportunity to create a more diverse and open society. The current government's attempts to integrate non-German residents into Germany is a major move in the creation of a new German identity, in line with the reality of a globalizing world.

The Changing Role of Women

Another major factor in the German Wertewandel is the changing role of women. As already discussed in chapter 5, there was a significant difference between the role of women in communist East Germany and that of women in the former states of West Germany. In former East Germany most women worked and enjoyed significant state support, in particular, free child-care facilities. Women in the east reject the idea of limiting the role of women to that of housewife, and many are angry about the losses they have incurred since reunification. Not only is child care no longer free, there are now twice as many unemployed women as men in former East Germany, and in 1996 birthrates were 60 percent lower than in 1989,[4] an ominous sign of population decline.

Traditionally in the west, being a *Hausfrau* (housewife) was a full-time job, including emotionally nurturing her husband and children as well as keeping the house clean and doing the shopping every day, sewing, cooking, and taking care of all the other myriad tasks that keep a household going. Typically, the Hausfrau was also responsible for caring for the old people (parents and in-laws) as age and illness made them unable to care for themselves. This system, while breaking down as more women enter the workforce, is still in place today, and there are only a limited number of homes for the aged in Germany. This fact should not be overly romanticized, however, because many of these older people are cared for in the home not as much out of love as to save financial resources.

This traditional system of the woman as service person dependent on the financial resources of the man is clearly undergoing major changes. More and more younger German women desire financial independence and a career path of their own. As they enter the workforce in increasing numbers, taking on occupations typically open in former times only to men, lifestyles and expectations are changing enormously. Certainly, many German working women are unhappy with having to do a "double shift," that is, having to put in a full day at work and then come home and still be responsible for all of the household duties.

This change in women's roles is a controversial topic in Germany, with conservative and progressive forces polarized around the issue. Although fairly progressive pregnancy leave policies are now law and the Green Party has made feminist concepts one of its central tenets, there is also a backlash among more conservative forces. Many Germans still believe that raising children is a full-time job and that at least one of the parents should forgo work outside the home to raise their children in a healthy and responsible manner.

Many middle-aged and older German women in the western states still elect to be full-time housewives and are accorded much respect. Even a significant portion of educated, younger German women, as stated in chapter 5, still choose to forgo a career in order to raise a family, but the declining birthrate in Germany indicates this group is becoming smaller. According to the *Economist*,[5] births per woman in Germany in 1999 were down to 1.3 from 2.4 in 1960. However, while Germans are having fewer babies, the percentage of women making up the total workforce has not changed as dramatically as in other countries. In 1960 women made up 35.3

percent of the workforce; today they account for only 41.3 percent. In the same years, women's employment in the United States rose from 25.5 percent to 46.5 percent.

Clearly, then, women's sense of identity and their role in life is changing. Today young German women are graduating from universities in increasingly high numbers, and they are less satisfied with filling traditional gender roles. Perhaps the once-commonly encountered proverb *Eine Frau ohne Mann ist wie ein Fisch ohne Fahrrad* (A woman without a man is like a fish without a bicycle) best illustrates the disenchantment of many younger German women as they struggle to work out of their traditional homebound situations.

But if traditional gender roles in Germany are breaking down, proper manners are still looked upon as a sign of a good upbringing. Holding the door for a woman or helping with a coat are just two examples of how Germans prefer more traditional behaviors to those of an androgynous neutrality. Like the French, they still seem to operate more on the principle of *vive la différence*.

New Lifestyles

These evolving women's roles are related to lifestyle changes in general among younger and some middle-aged Germans. Changing family structures and child-rearing practices reflect the trends toward stronger democracy, a more global perspective, and expanding individualism in Germany. Since the late 1960s these changes have continued to gain strength and momentum. And like so many aspects of life in Germany, they have strong ideological, political, and financial consequences, making them subjects of animated public debate.

One of the issues at the heart of this debate is the tax and social security advantages given to married couples. Because an increasing number of younger couples have chosen to forgo an official marriage and are simply living together, they are unhappy with what they view as economic discrimination. These so-called *"wilde Ehe"* (common law marriages) are becoming more common and are only one dimension of a growing number of lifestyle changes among Germans who choose not to live in a traditional family structure. As throughout much of Europe, more and more Germans are not only postponing marriage but are also pushing back the age at which they decide to have children. While the birthrate is decreasing, divorce rates and the number of singles living alone are rising.

There are also a growing number of *Wohngemeinschaften* (communal housing units). These "WGs" are a form of group living in which a number of people live together as a small community that substitutes for the traditional family. Generally, persons living in WGs tend to be young and liberal, and their lifestyles and personal constellations as well as their forms of partnership vary significantly. To see just how popular these new communal living forms are, one need only look in the telephone directory of staid old Stuttgart. There you will find one whole page listing only WGs.

Regarding sexual matters, Germans are typically quite matter-of-fact, viewing the subject more as a matter of biology than morality, and their educational system reinforces this view. German schools have been offering *Sexualkunde* (sex education) classes since the early part of this century, and today German pupils will typically have had three coed classes in sex education before leaving school.

This is not to say that some Germans are not prudish, but typically Germans find it easier to talk more openly about sexual matters than do people from other cultures. This is certainly confirmed by the creative public advertising campaigns encouraging Germans to use condoms to stop the spread of the HIV virus. Similarly, nudity is considered quite normal in Germany, and nude beaches and coed saunas are common throughout the country. Foreign tourists are typically left staring upon finding themselves surrounded by nude sunbathers in downtown Munich's beautiful English Garden.

Print and mass media in Germany are also liberal in their portrayals of human nudity, and most Germans think little of this. Typically they find sex and nudity far less threatening than violence. They often question why parents in the United States allow their children to watch so much violence and killing on television, yet get disturbed about nudity or sex. Like many Europeans, Germans do not find sexual explicitness problematic as long as it is portrayed in an aesthetic manner.

And like many Europeans, Germans view sexual matters as an intimate part of one's private sphere. The focus of American media on the Bill Clinton-Monica Lewinsky affair and subsequent impeachment process left them aghast. They simply could not understand why a public official's private affairs were being dragged out onto the public stage. Because of their more matter-of-fact approach to sex and their belief in the rights of all individuals to a private life, they found America's fascination with the Clinton affair incomprehensible.

Perhaps because of their more biological approach to sexual matters, platonic relationships between male and female Germans are fairly common. It is not uncommon for Germans to socialize with members of the opposite sex, even when no direct romantic interest is involved. In general, American-style dating is less prevalent in Germany, where people still tend to meet and socialize more in group settings. This group orientation is supported by German *Kneipenkultur* (pub culture), which encourages meetings between people in the cafes, bars, and beer gardens found throughout the country.

Changes in Child Raising

For those Germans who do choose to have children, there is a clear trend toward having fewer children and bearing them later in life. This is undoubtedly the result of more Germans deciding to emphasize their personal and career development rather than raising a family early in life.

The trend toward individualistic lifestyles is in marked contrast to previous generations. Traditional Germans felt it was their duty to marry and raise children to be well-disciplined, obedient, and subordinate. The traditional authoritarian style of raising children to be disciplined and obedient fit well with the rigid class society of the German Empire as well as with the fascist ideology of the Nazis. It also supported an ethos that saw the state as a guardian of the people, who willingly accepted their consequent lack of individual freedom. More and more Germans now see their task as raising their children to be more autonomous and self-reliant.[6] Today's children are also being taught to be far more tolerant than previous generations. Today, most Germans agree that what Germany needs most is *mündiger Bürger* (responsible citizens), that is, citizens who are well educated and informed, independent thinkers who actively take part in Germany's sociopolitical processes. These changes in attitude clearly reflect Germans' coming to terms with their authoritarian past and their attempts to support and fortify their already stable democracy. Today a major public debate centers around this tension between the role of the state and the growth of individual freedoms and rights of citizens to structure their lives as they choose.

That these younger Germans are different from older generations can be seen in various other aspects of life in Germany, in addition to changes in women's roles, marriage patterns, and child raising. Because they are less obedient and less willing to give in to authoritarian pressure, their teachers, managers, and employers are being forced to revise the way they have traditionally operated. Classes in German schools are far less authoritarian than previously, and many older pupils now openly question their teachers' opinions and teachings. Similarly, when they enter the workforce, these younger Germans have less patience with authoritarian bosses and are more willing to complain about it. Managers who once had only to give orders must now be ready with explanations when younger employees call their decisions into question.

As these younger Germans mature without having experienced the hardships and material deprivations of previous generations, they also tend to be less risk-aversive than their parents. This change is clearly signaled by the growing number who are investing in the more risky stock markets, compared with previous generations who would never have considered putting their money anywhere else but in a savings account. And younger Germans seem more willing to move from the security of their home regions if their careers demand it.

Individuation and Amerikanisierung

The notion of the *Amerikanisierung* (Americanization) of Germany is widespread among Germans, and the term itself is frequently heard. It incorporates the idea that whatever happens in the United States will spread to Germany a few years later. Ask Germans for proof of this phenomenon and most will immediately point to the large number of English words that continue to enter the German language as well as the styles of clothing and music preferred by younger Germans, not to mention the profusion of American fast-food restaurants throughout the country. The idea of Amerikanisierung also refers to less superficial aspects of cultural transfer, such as the growing poverty, homelessness, and crime rates, which cause all Germans great worry. How ubiquitous this Amerikanisierung of Germany is can be illustrated by the theme of a recent convention of German urban centers, "The Americanization of the Cities."

The United States has influenced Germany enormously since 1945. The occupation by the Allies and the denazification process they instigated allowed the forces of German democracy to reemerge and take root in more fertile soil than ever before. The Marshall Plan provided financial aid for socioeconomic development, giving this democratization process an improved basis for success. Rather than allow hatred and desire for revenge to gain the upper hand as they had at the end of World War I, this more enlightened approach put in movement a process of change that continues to this day.

Along with the democratization process came a clear trend toward increased individualism. There are many signs that Germans are moving away from their traditional group-oriented culture toward a more individualistic society. This individuation process is another major component of the Wertewandel, and one that not all Germans are happy with. Some signs of the growing individualism are, as I noted earlier, the rise in the divorce rate, the expansion of the singles scene, a decline in the attachment to the family, and increased interest in self-development and personal growth. The New Age movement is also finding numerous converts in Germany.

Because younger Germans have been raised in a less authoritarian style than previous generations, they seem more willing to structure their lives according to their own needs and desires and less on the dictates of the group. Closely aligned with this trend is the desire of many younger Germans for a less formal life where *soziale Zwänge* (social pressures and conventions) play less of a role. The experiments of younger Germans with new lifestyles and living arrangements often dismay their more conservative compatriots. One of the common complaints heard from more traditional Germans is that Germany has become more *egoistisch* (egotistical) and that fewer and fewer people are willing to put the common good ahead of their own personal needs and desires. Much of this is viewed as a result of the Amerikanisierung of Germany.

And the influence of the United States continues to grow. This can be seen in the enduring German fascination with American films and television programs. In fact, the broadcast of the American television series *Holocaust* was a major event in Germany during the late 1970s, setting off another wave of critical debate and self-reflection regarding its Nazi past. More recently, *Schindler's List* was a box-office hit and served to keep fresh the public discussion about the country's past. Today a wide variety of American entertainment can be seen on German television. In addition, American (and English) rock music is almost as popular in Germany as it is in the U.S. Similarly, the youth of Germany readily take to the clothing styles they see first on their U.S. counterparts.

The media and the constant traffic between Germany and the United States also support the growing influence of English on the German language. English words such as *meeting, date, small talk, rap music, teamwork, coaching,* and so forth are now quite common in the speech of many Germans, so much so that many people have begun to refer to this style of peppering sentences with English words as *Neudeutsch* (new German). This "Englishization" is unintentionally supported by the German school curriculum, which requires all German pupils to begin learning English in the fourth or fifth grade.

In addition to the political, media, and pop-culture influences, American business theories and practices are also a major component in the *Amerikanisierung* of Germany. Many American companies have set up operations in Germany, while, at the same time, German companies have also entered the American market.

German industry has recently been caught up in a wave of corporate restructuring. The adoption by Daimler-Benz of American-style accounting procedures and its subsequent listing on the New York Stock Exchange as well as the hostile takeover attempt of Thyssen by Krupp are only two examples that illustrate that it is not business as usual in Germany today. A lively public discussion is currently taking place in Germany as to whether the German social market economic model, with its cornerstones of consensus among political parties, employers, and the unions along with an expensive social welfare system will be able to keep Germany productive and competitive in the globalizing world market. Many voices are calling for strengthening this system to maintain social peace and stability. Others, however, argue that it is imperative for Germany to adopt a freer, more aggressive American style of capitalism with its hire-and-fire tactics in order to remain viable economically.

Changes in Education

Even Germany's hallowed educational system is showing signs of fatigue and is currently the subject of loud criticism. Calls for reform are rampant, but to date all parties involved—government, faculty, administration, and students—have done little beyond attempt to place the blame elsewhere.

Germany's universities were originally designed to educate a relatively small number of elite students, and they served their purpose well. But since World War II, as Germany has become more democratic and its economy has needed more highly educated employees, the numbers of students entering the university has grown enormously. Its once-respected universities are now overcrowded, and in 1997 ever-worsening conditions sparked Germany's largest student protests in thirty years. Today approximately 1.9 million students are crowded into a system designed to accommodate only 950,000.[7] Despite a universally acknowledged need for university reform, entrenched bureaucracies, financial crisis, and government incompetence have allowed for only minor tinkering with a system in need of a major overhaul.

In recent years a spate of private universities has opened in response to the need, offering courses in business, management, and economics. Parallel to this development, some of the public universities have begun to charge tuition for courses of study that are open only to a limited number of students and where services are better. If there is no significant reform in higher education, expect these two trends to continue.

At the other end of the scale, far fewer young people are entering the vocational educational tracks. At the same time, fewer companies seem willing or able to foot the expenses for training apprentices. These two trends may ultimately have serious consequences for this small nation, which has made up for its lack of natural resources by having a highly trained workforce.

While all of these economic, political, and social forces are transforming Germany as it enters the twenty-first century, long-standing forces are also exerting influence.

A Search for Roots

Germany was recently confronted with the fiftieth anniversary of the major events surrounding the end of World War II. During that period I had the privilege of being in Germany to do field research for my dissertation. One bright sunny day, I went to the doctor for a minor medical problem. As I left her office and turned the corner to walk into the square, I found my way blocked by uniformed police. When I asked an officer what was happening, I was surprised to discover the entire area had been cordoned off because of a bomb scare. My first thought was terrorists, but as I continued asking questions, I found the source of the bomb to be a real surprise.

In the course of digging up a street, construction workers had stumbled upon an unexploded American bomb that had been dropped during World War II. Finding unexploded bombs, shells, and hand grenades is becoming less frequent in Germany, but it still happens. After the area had been evacuated, a bomb crew was called in to defuse the bomb. Although I was intellectually aware of how much the events of World War II still influenced Germans, I had never felt that impact so viscerally before.

For many Germans the war is a source of profound guilt, and they often find it hard to be patriotic or to develop a positive national identity. Because of this guilt, some identify more closely with their local region than they do with the country or tend to think of themselves as "Europeans" or even citizens of the world. Many would simply like to forget the war and move on. This is especially true of younger Germans born thirty and forty years after the war ended and who find it annoying to still be held accountable for the deeds of their grandparents. All of this makes the German preoccupation with Vergangenheitsbewältigung (coming to terms with the past) and Heimat unique.

Heimat is a strange word in German. As John Ardagh[8] points out, it literally means "home" or "homeland," but it has far deeper emotional meanings for Germans. For them it is less a physical place and more a state of mind, a sense of nostalgia, and a yearning for belonging. Because the Nazis misused this word in their propaganda campaigns, as they did so many other core German words, many people felt a strong inhibition against using this word after the war. Since 1945 great portions of German culture and achievements were in some way denounced or called into question. At first Germans denied much of their past history, which created a sort of collective amnesia, and the word Heimat was rarely used in any positive sense by liberal or progressive Germans. This selective amnesia about and denial of their past resulted in a great cultural gap, which made Germans feel cut off from their historical and cultural roots while suffering under heavy guilt and carrying the burden of a distinctly negative national identity. But as the trauma and mistakes of the past are acknowledged and processed, this cultural rupture has begun to heal.

While not wishing to repeat the mistakes and excesses of what has gone before, more and more Germans are able to reconnect with their cultural roots and take pride in the positive aspects of their rich heritage. Thus we see an almost paradoxical development in Germany today. On the one hand, Germans are becoming more world-minded and tolerant, and on the other, they are finding their way toward more self-acceptance and pride in their culture's historical achievements as well as current accomplishments. Both are directly related to Vergangenheitsbewältigung.

The Twenty-First Century

Like most nations around the world, Germany is undergoing rapid and profound changes. The coming of the information age, the globalization of the world economy, and the consolidation and expansion of the European Union are just some of the major external changes to which Germany is struggling to adjust. Internally, as we have discussed in this chapter, Germany is becoming more individualistic and more diverse. Traditional gender roles are changing, as are lifestyles and attitudes. And basic political, economic, and social institutions are being critically examined and subjected to pressures for reform.

These are only a few of the many changes facing Germany at the turn of the century. Many of these challenges are large and will directly impact Germans and the way they organize and structure their lives for decades to come. But given their important central position in Europe and their previous phoenixlike resurrections, we can safely assume that the Germans will provide fascinating solutions to these difficult challenges and problems. As Americans, we will do well to watch our German friends in order to learn from and with them.

---

[1] Barbara Beck, "Germany's Chance to Be Different," *The World in 1999* (London: Economist Publications, 1998), 49.

[2] It also accounts for much of the alienation and rightist extremism among the youth in the eastern states.

[3] "Turkish Germans?" *Economist*, 9 January 1999, 17.

[4] "Wozu die Quälerei?" *Der Spiegel* 43 (1996): 86.

[5] Barbara Beck, "Executive, Thy Name Is Woman," *The World in 1999* (London: Economist Publications, 1998), 89.

[6] Thomas Gensicke, "Wertewandel und Familie," *Aus Politik und Zeitgeschichte—Beilage zur Wochenzeitung Das Parlament*, B29-30/94 (22 July 1994): 39.

[7] Andrea Schulte-Peevers, "Are German Students Missing the Boat?" *German Life* (August/September 1998): 38–41.

[8] John Ardagh, *Germany and the Germans*, 3d ed. (Hammondsworth, England: Penguin Books, 1995), 348.

Appendix

Statistical Comparison of Germany and the United States

	United States	**Germany**
Area	3,536,341 sq. mi.	137,803 sq. mi.
Population	269,816,000	82,079,454
Population Density	76 per sq. mi.	596 per sq. mi.
Birthrate	14.4/1000	8.8/1000
Religion	Protestant 61% Roman Catholic 25% Jewish 2% Other 5% None 7%	Protestant 38% Roman Catholic 34% Muslims 1.7% Unaffiliated or other 26.3%
Gross Domestic Product	$7.61 trillion	$1.7 trillion
GDP per capita income	$28,600	$20,400

All data from the *Time Almanac* 1999 (Information Please, LLC: Boston, MA).

Glossary of German Terms

Abitur. University Entrance Qualification; the graduation certificate awarded after passing a rigorous set of exams at the end of academic high school education. *See* Gymnasium.

abstimmen. To vote or decide.

alles klar. Everything is okay.

Amerikanisierung. The Americanization of Germany, which refers to American-influenced changes to German values, society, and lifestyle since the end of World War II.

Aufklärung. Enlightenment, the historical period and philosophical position in Europe that stresses the paramount value of rational and objective thought for solving personal and societal problems.

aufrecht. Upright; of good character.

Aufsichtsrat. Supervisory board in large corporations.

Bekannte. Acquaintances; Americans might use the word *friends*, while Germans make a clearer distinction. *See* Freunde.

bestimmt auftreten. To speak and behave in a self-confident manner; for Germans, this means an air of calm resolve and an aura of no nonsense.

Betriebsrat. Works council; body in German business organizations representing the interests of both blue-collar and white-collar employees.

BRD. Abbreviation for *Bundesrepublik Deutschland,* the Federal Republic of Germany (FRG), that is, former West Germany as well as the name for reunified Germany.

Bundestag. German parliament.

Bürgertum. Professional and commercial middle class, in traditional class society.

Chefsekretärin. Head secretary, personal assistant, and "right hand" of a high-level manager.

Datenschutzgesetz. Law that protects individuals from the collection and storage of data for commercial or government use.

DDR. Abbreviation for *Deutsche Demokratische Republik,* the German Democratic Republic (GDR), in other words, former East Germany.

deuten. To explain, interpret.

deutlich. Clear, plain, distinct.

Deutsch. The German language.

deutsche Mark (DM). The name of Germany's unit of currency, the German mark.

Deutschland. Germany. *See BRD and DDR.*

Dienst ist Dienst und Schnaps ist Schnaps. (literally, Duty is duty and liquor is liquor.) Duty and pleasure should not be mixed.

Diskussion. Discussion.

Eine Frau ohne Mann ist wie ein Fisch ohne Fahrrad. A woman without a man is like a fish without a bicycle.

Einwohnermeldeamt. Registration office for residents; both Germans and non-Germans are obliged by law to register their place of residence with this office upon arrival in the locality.

Erziehung. One's upbringing, manners, education.

Erziehungsurlaub. Unpaid parental leave.

Fasching. Boisterous pre-Lent celebration comparable to Mardi Gras.

Frauenförderungsprogramme. Programs for the advancement of women in business or public service; frequently this includes a quota system for women's job promotions.

Freunde. Friends; for Germans, this means close, personal, long-standing relationships. See Bekannte.

Gastarbeiter. Guest worker(s); mostly Italian, Spanish, Greek, and Turkish nationals working in German industry.

Gemeinschaft. Community, ingroup with a sense of shared responsibility for the common good.

gemütlich. Cozy, congenial, jolly, hearty.

Gemütlichkeit. Term which typically applies to the private sphere, describing a sense of coziness, warmth, or a convivial atmosphere

Gründlichkeit. Thoroughness; in-depth, detail-oriented mode of working.

Grundschule. Basic elementary school.

Gruppenzugehörigkeit. Sense of belonging to or being part of a group.

Gymnasium. Academic high school, the academically most rigorous track in German secondary education. Gymnasium ends with the Abitur, when pupils are eighteen or nineteen years old and have completed a total of thirteen years of schooling.

Hauptschule. Academically the least demanding track of secondary education in Germany. Hauptschule ends after a total of nine years of formal education, when pupils are fifteen or sixteen years old.

Hausfrau. Housewife.

Heimat. Home, roots, deep sense of local or emotional belonging.

Hochdeutsch. High German; standard German.

IHK. Abbreviation for *Industrie und Handelskammern*, Chambers of Industry and Commerce.

Kaffee und Kuchen. German tradition of serving coffee and cake (often homemade) in the afternoon.

Kehrwoche. Round-robin system in which weekly cleaning tasks are assigned to residents of apartments (literally, sweeping week).

Kern. The core, essence, or true nature of a person; a problem, a musical theme, and so on.

Kinder, Küche, Kirche. Literally, "Children, kitchen, church," a reactionary saying implying that women should not venture out beyond their traditional, subservient roles.

Klare Rechnung, gute Freundschaft. Clear bill (when all is explicitly clear), good friendship.

Klarheit. Clarity; refers to an unambiguous stance regarding a given topic, as well as to people who are precise in their thinking and straightforward in speaking their mind.

Klartext. Clearly, directly.

Kneipenkultur. German pub culture; Germans do much of their socializing in pubs (Kneipen), and the country has an astounding variety of them.

Land. State.

mitarbeiten. To work together.

mitbestimmen. To codetermine.

Mitbestimmung. Codetermination; industrial democracy.

mitdenken. To think along the same lines.

mitreden. To have the right or duty to speak out.

mitwirken. To participate in.

Mittelstand. Small and medium-sized companies in Germany.

mündiger Bürger. Responsible citizen; citizen capable of independent thinking and democratic outlook.

Nachkriegsgeneration. Generation of Germans who lived through and were shaped by the harsh period directly after World War II.

Neudeutsch. Literally, "new German"; a word used to mean the many changes currently taking place in the German language, in particular the wide use of English words.

Ordnung. Order, structure, appropriateness, tidiness, and much more; a belief in "a place for everything and everything in its place"; a key concept for Germans.

Ordnung müß sein. There must be order.

Ossis. Colloquial, sometimes slightly derogatory term used for East Germans since reunification (literally, Easterners).

Pflichtbewußtsein. Awareness of one's obligations and duties, particularly in regard to the good of the overall group.

Rabenmutter. A mother who neglects her duties toward her children (literally, raven mother).

Realschule. Middle track of secondary education in Germany; ends after a total of ten years of school education.

Ruhetag. "Rest day"; refers mainly to Sundays when all shops are closed. It can also refer to a set day in the week when a particular restaurant or bar is not open for business.

sachlich. Relevant, pertinent.

Sachlichkeit. Matter-of-factness; content-focused mode of speech and communication.

Sexualkunde. Sex education.

sich zu blamieren. To cause one's disgrace.

soziale Marktwirtschaft. Social market economy; capitalism with a human face—the economic system in the Federal Republic of Germany.

soziale Partner. Social partners; in other words, management and labor.

soziale Zwänge. Social conventions or pressures on behavior, in particular an emphasis on constraint and conformity.

sportiv. Gamelike.

Stammtisch. Table reserved for regulars in a German restaurant or pub.

Stimme. Voice.

Stunde Null. Zero hour; end of World War II.

Sturm und Drang. An influential period in German literature and philosophy advocating a deeply emotional, romantic ideal. Before entering their classical periods, both Goethe and Schiller were proponents of this outlook on life (literally, tempest and desire).

sympathisch. Likable, pleasant.

Treuhandanstalt. Institute of Trustees; in other words, the organization that was in charge of the divestment and restructuring process of East German industry after the reunification of Germany.

Trümmerfrauen. Those women who rebuilt much of Germany's housing that had been destroyed during World War II (literally, women of the rubble).

TÜV. Abbreviation for *Technischer Überwachungsverein,* a German institution in charge of safety standards for cars and other technical equipment.

überschwenglich. Excessively exuberant.

unter uns. "Amongst ourselves," a term used by Germans to refer to communication with members of an ingroup.

Unterhaltung. A word that means both entertainment and conversation.

unverschämt teuer. Shamelessly expensive.

verbindlich. Binding, obligatory, or compulsory.

Verbindlichkeit. Awareness and fulfillment of social or economic obligation. This term has positive connotations in German and is also used to describe reliability.

Vergangenheitsbewältigung. Understanding, coming to terms with, and atoning for the horrors of Nazi fascism and World War II (literally, dealing with the past).

Vernunft. Ability to use one's intellectual capacities to arrive at a balanced and moderate position; the opposite would be irrationality or being unreasonable.

vertiefen. To deepen; that is, to go into more depth and detail, particularly when discussing an issue or when developing relationships.

Vorstand. Executive or management board in large business corporations.

Wanderlust. The desire to roam or wander, often used to describe Germans' extensive travels abroad during vacations, particularly during the summer months.

Wende (die Wende). The turning point in recent German history; refers to the reunification of Germany in 1989–1990.

Wertewandel. The changes in German values, society, and lifestyles since the 1960s (literally, value change).

Wessis. Colloquial, sometimes slightly derogatory term used for West Germans since reunification (literally, Westerners).

wilde Ehe. Colloquial term for unmarried couples living together.

Wirtschaftswunder. Germany's economic miracle; the amazing economic recovery in the 1950s and 1960s, which made Germany one of the leading economies in the world after the destruction in World War II.

Wissenschaft. Science and technology, a rational approach to life.

Wohngemeinschaft. Communal living.

Zusammenbruch. Breakdown of Germany; a period of great material, emotional, and psychological suffering after World War II.

References and Further Readings

"Adored No More." *Economist*, 21 March 1998, 84.

Allen, William Sheridan. *The Nazi Seizure of Power*. New York: New Viewpoints, 1973.

Allianz AG, Annual Report, 1997.

"Allianz—A Wholly German Empire?" *Economist*, 2 November 1991, 77–78.

Ardagh, John. *Germany and the Germans*. 3d ed. Hammondsworth, England: Penguin Books, 1995.

Barbour, Stephen, and Patrick Stevenson. *Variation in German*. Cambridge: Cambridge University Press, 1990.

Beck, Barbara. "Germany's Chance to Be Different." *The World in 1999* (London: Economist Publications, 1998), 48–49.

———. "Executive, Thy Name Is Woman." *The World in 1999* (London: Economist Publications, 1998), 89.

Burns, Robert. *German Cultural Studies—An Introduction*. Oxford: Oxford University Press, 1995.

Byrnes, Heidi. "Interactional Styles in German and American Conversations." *Text* 6, no. 2 (1986): 189–206.

Clyne, Michael. *Language and Society in the German-Speaking Countries*. Cambridge: Cambridge University Press, 1984.

Craig, Gordon A. *Germany 1866–1945*. London: Oxford University Press, 1984.

———. *The Germans*. New York: New American Library, 1983.

———. *The Politics of the Prussian Army, 1640–1945*. London: Oxford University Press, 1955.

"Dieser Krieg läßt uns alle nicht los." *Die Zeit*, 13, 28 March 1997, 16.

Doing Business in Eastern Germany. One of a series of excellent articles on investing in Eastern Germany. Available from the American Chamber of Commerce, 12 Rossmarkt, Frankfurt/Main.

Dundes, Alan. *Life Is Like a Chicken Coop Ladder*. Detroit: Wayne State University Press, 1984.

Elias, Norbert. *Studien über die Deutschen: Machtkämpfe und Habitusentwicklung im 19. und 20. Jahrhundert*. Frankfurt/Main: Suhrkamp Taschenbuch Verlag, 1994.

Flippo, Hyde. *The German Way*. Lincolnwood, IL: Passport Books, 1997.

Foster, George. "Peasant Society and the Image of Limited Good." *American Anthropolgist* 67, no. 2 (April 1965): 293–315.

Friday, Robert. "Contrasts in Discussion Behaviors of German and American Managers." *International Journal of Intercultural Relations* 13, no. 4 (1989): 429–45.

Gensicke, Thomas. "Wertewandel und Familie." *Aus Politik und Zeitgeschichte—Beilage zur Wochenzeitung Das Parlament*, B29-30/94 (22 July 1994).

"German Banking's Industrial Revolution," *Economist*, 19 December 1998, 106.

Glouchevitch, Philip. *Juggernaut: The German Way of Business*. New York: Simon & Schuster, 1992.

Hall, Edward T., and Mildred Reed Hall. *Hidden Differences: How to Communicate with the Germans*. Hamburg, Germany: Stern Press, 1983.

Hampden-Turner, Charles, and Fons Trompenaars. *The Seven Cultures of Capitalism*. New York: Doubleday, 1993.

Haney, C., and Philip G. Zimbardo. "The Socialization into Criminality: On Becoming a Prisoner and a Guard." In *Law, Justice and the Individual in Society: Pyschological and Legal Issues*, edited by J. L. Tapp and F. L. Levine, 198–223. New York: Holt, Rinehart & Winston, 1977.

Hardt, Hanno. "Communication and Economic Thought: Cultural Imagination in German and American Scholarship." *Communication* 10 (1988): 141–64.

Kalberg, Stephen. "West German and American Interaction Forms: One Level of Structured Misunderstanding." *Theory, Culture & Society* 4 (1987): 603–18.

Kramer, Dieter. *German Holidays and Folk Customs*. Bonn: Atlantik Brücke, 1986.

Lewin, Kurt: "Some Social-Psychological Differences between the United States and Germany." *Character and Personality* 4 (1936): 265–93.

Lord, Richard. *Culture Shock Germany: A Guide to Customs and Etiquette*. Portland, OR: Graphic Arts Center Publishing, 1996.

"Metall Bashing." *Economist*, 19 February 1994, 15–16.

Milgram, Stanley. *Obedience to Authority*. New York: Harper & Row, 1974.

"New Dreams at Deutsche Bank." *Economist*, 22 June 1991, 79–81.

"Ohne Kerle." *Manager Magazin*, November 1998, 359–64.

Pasley, Malcolm. *Germany—A Companion to German Studies*. London: Methuen, 1972.

Pinzler, Petra. "Kinder, Küche, Karriereknicke." *Die Zeit—Wirtschaft Spezial*, 43, October 1996, 33–34.

Press and Information Office of the Federal Government. *Facts about Germany*. Frankfurt/Main: Societäts Verlag, 1997.

Reinhardt, Kurt F. *Germany: 2000 Years*, vol. 1. New York: Frederick Ungar Publishing, 1966.

Rommel, Günter, et al. *Simplicity Wins: How Germany's Mid-Sized Companies Succeed.* Boston: Harvard Business School Press, 1995.

"Saving the German Way." *Europe,* November 1992, 39–40.

Schäfgen, Katrin, and Annette Spellerberg. "Kulturelle Leitbilder und institutionelle Regelungen für Frauen in den USA, in West—und in Ostdeutschland." *Berliner Journal für Soziologie* 1 (1998): 73–90.

Schroll-Machl, Sylvia. "Die Zusammenarbeit in internationalen Teams—Eine interkulturelle Herausforderung dargestellt am Beispiel USA-Deutschland." In *Internationales Change Management,* edited by Jörg M. Scholz. Stuttgart: Schäffer-Poeschel Verlag, 1995.

Schulte-Peevers, Andrea. "Are German Students Missing the Boat?" *German Life,* August/September 1998, 38–41.

Simon, Hermann. *Hidden Champions: Lessons from 500 of the World's Best Unknown Companies.* Boston: Harvard Business School Press, 1996.

Stern, Susan. *These Strange German Ways.* Bonn: Atlantik-Bruecke, 1994.

Tillier, Alan. *Doing Business in Today's Western Europe.* Lincolnwood, IL: NTC Business Books, 1992.

Tinnappel, Friederike. "Ein Potential, das Firmen langsam entdecken." *Frankfurter Rundschau,* 18 October 1996.

Tolzmann, Don H. "The German American Legacy." *German Life* 1, June/July 1994, 46–49.

Trompenaars, Fons. *Riding the Waves of Culture.* London: Irwin Professional Publishing, 1994.

"Turkish Germans?" *Economist,* 9 January 1999, 17.

"Vorwärts in der Vergangenheit." *Der Spiegel,* 23, 1995, 72–82.

Watson, Alan. *The Germans: Who Are They Now?* London: Mandarin Paperbacks, 1995.

Weber, Max. *The Protestant Ethic and the Spirit of Capitalism.* London, George Allen & Unwin, 1976.

"Wozu die Quälerei?" *Der Spiegel* 43, 1996, 78–111.

Zusammen leben mit Ausländern. Bonn: Inter Nationes, 1995.

Index

A

E

K

L

O

P